T0380714

REDIRECT

A FREEDOM PLAN FROM PORNOGRAPHY'S CONTROL

DOUG R.CONDER, PH.D. w/ REES J. CONDER

WESTBOW
PRESS®
A DIVISION OF THOMAS NELSON
& ZONDERVAN

Copyright © 2024 Doug R.Conder, Ph.D. w/ Rees J. Conder.

All rights reserved. No part of this book may be used or reproduced by any means, graphic, electronic, or mechanical, including photocopying, recording, taping or by any information storage retrieval system without the written permission of the author except in the case of brief quotations embodied in critical articles and reviews.

This book is a work of non-fiction. Unless otherwise noted, the author and the publisher make no explicit guarantees as to the accuracy of the information contained in this book and in some cases, names of people and places have been altered to protect their privacy.

WestBow Press books may be ordered through booksellers or by contacting:

WestBow Press
A Division of Thomas Nelson & Zondervan
1663 Liberty Drive
Bloomington, IN 47403
www.westbowpress.com
844-714-3454

Because of the dynamic nature of the Internet, any web addresses or links contained in this book may have changed since publication and may no longer be valid. The views expressed in this work are solely those of the author and do not necessarily reflect the views of the publisher, and the publisher hereby disclaims any responsibility for them.

Any people depicted in stock imagery provided by Getty Images are models, and such images are being used for illustrative purposes only. Certain stock imagery © Getty Images.

ISBN: 979-8-3850-2836-8 (sc)
ISBN: 979-8-3850-2837-5 (hc)
ISBN: 979-8-3850-2838-2 (e)

Library of Congress Control Number: 2024912652

Print information available on the last page.

WestBow Press rev. date: 10/14/2024

Scripture taken from the *Amplified Bible*, copyright © 1954, 1958, 1962, 1964, 1965, 1987 by The Lockman Foundation. Used by permission.

Scripture quotations taken from the New American Standard Bible®, Copyright © 1960, 1962, 1963, 1968, 1971, 1972, 1973, 1975, 1977, 1995 by The Lockman Foundation. Used by permission. (www.Lockman.org)

Scripture taken from the New King James Version. Copyright © 1979, 1980, 1982 by Thomas Nelson, Inc. Used by permission. All rights reserved.

Scripture quotations taken from the Holy Bible, New Living Translation, Copyright © 1996, 2004. Used by permission of Tyndale House Publishers, Inc., Wheaton, Illinois 60189. All rights reserved.

Scripture taken from the Holy Bible, NEW INTERNATIONAL VERSION®. Copyright © 1973, 1978, 1984, 2011 by Biblica, Inc. All rights reserved worldwide. Used by permission. NEW INTERNATIONAL VERSION® and NIV® are registered trademarks of Biblica, Inc. Use of either trademark for the offering of goods or services requires the prior written consent of Biblica US, Inc.

Scripture quotations marked TPT are from The Passion Translation®. Copyright © 2017, 2018, 2020 by Passion & Fire Ministries, Inc. Used by permission. All rights reserved. ThePassionTranslation.com.

CONTENTS

To the love of my life, Kimberly, the most loving and encouraging wife ever. Thank you for your unflinching support for this project and the years of patiently waiting.

FOREWORD

Dear Friend,

There is hope!

"So if the Son sets you free, you really will be free" (John 8:36 NASB).

I am eternally grateful for the cross of Jesus Christ. Where would we all be if Jesus did not reach down to us, choosing us while we were still in sin, claiming us as His very own, covering us with His precious blood, washing and forgiving us, and making us brand-new? We would all be lost.

But God! We have been brought close by His precious blood!

Thank You, Jesus for the blood applied
Thank You, Jesus it has washed me white
Thank You, Jesus You have saved my life

Brought me from the darkness into glorious light.

> Charity Gayle, "Thank You Jesus for the Blood" *Endless Praise* (2021, Apple Music)

What can wash away my sin?
Nothing but the blood of Jesus.
What can make me whole again?
Nothing but the blood of Jesus.

> Robert Lowry, "Nothing But the Blood of Jesus" (1876, public domain)

It's under this blood that we stand totally and completely forgiven. We have been made free!

I live with a man who has been free from the demons of pornography for decades, my precious Douglas. He is my favorite human on earth, my best friend, the most tender, selfless, wise, Spirit-led person I know-- and I get to be married to him! I definitely got the better end of this deal.

Shortly, you'll read his story and those of others like him who have found these truths:

1. Jesus really is alive, and He overcame all the works of the devil, including pornography.
2. His Spirit is at work, and it fills us with a power that is greater than anything on earth, in hell, or the grave, He fills us with Himself!
3. The Word of God—the Bible—is living and active (Hebrews 4:12–13 NASB). "Submit yourselves then to God. Resist the devil, and he will flee from you. Come near to God and He will come near to you" (James 4:7–8 NIV).

Friend, you will learn what God taught Doug. These are stories, examples, and tools for your freedom journey that you can implement immediately. These have been valuable treasures of the kingdom that Doug has found. I've watched as he has sold everything he has—his reputation, influence, and formal career ambitions—to buy the field (Matthew 13:44 NKJV). For Doug, this is what the Lord asked of him, and I am so grateful for his obedience. I am aware, to the extent that I know, of the (we will say) countless number of men he spends his daily time with. Every day a call, an email, a text, a visit, a coffee, a lunch, a late-night FaceTime, etc. Doug's freedom isn't regulated to Sundays or when he is invited to a men's retreat, small group, conference, Bible class, or speaking engagement. His freedom is not a switch he flips on or off—it is who he is because it is Christ, who is living by His Spirit through him.

Jesus didn't want us to stay inside the church building when He busted down the gates of hell and destroyed sin and the grave for us. I've lost count of how many times Doug and I have been standing in line for something and Doug starts up a conversation with the man behind us, and before long, I glance back and see Doug is praying for the guy who is now on the verge of tears. Or Doug saying to me at the airport, "Sweetie, I'll be back in just a few minutes. I'm going over there to talk to that guy." Or the times when I've looked across the room at weddings and funerals (literally) to find Doug with his hand on a man's shoulder as he is crying, and Doug is praying and prophesying life into him. This also happens at restaurants, while we are shopping, on the golf course, in parking lots, on vacations, while we're walking our dog, or getting the truck washed— you get the picture. Anywhere and everywhere.

I've watched him give up sleep at night to assist in praying the Word of God through the night for some struggling brother's breakthrough to freedom. He has flown across the country and driven mile after mile to go after other brothers who are fighting addiction.

Why do I tell you these things? *Not* for you to think highly of Doug—he is just a man—but to think highly of Christ, who lives in Doug.

> For Christ's love compels us. (2 Corinthians 5:14 NIV)

The point is freedom will do *whatever* is necessary.

> It was for freedom that Christ has set us free. (Galatians 5:1 NASB)

The second voice you will read periodically throughout this book is that of another man who has been transformed and made new—our son, Rees. Rees, like his dad, is a man of joy and integrity. His honesty, passion, and wisdom are compelling. His contribution is inspiring and will bless you greatly.

Friend, you are being prayed for. We may not know your name, but He does. There is hope, much hope. May your heart rest in Him, for you are tenderly and affectionately loved right now, right where you are, in the midst of your pit or mountaintop, or somewhere in between. He sees you, knows you, and loves you. You do not need to hide any longer. Come and find freedom. Come and find hope.

From a fellow freedom finder,
Kimberly Conder

ACKNOWLEDGMENTS

There have been many encouraging voices along the way with this project, and at the beginning of each day, we all need that type of support, don't we! Thank you, Chris and Tara, Chris and Kim, Michael and Lorisa, Matt and Jana, Asus and Mimi. Thank you also to our Blue River Woods small group, our LifeMission church home group, the CEC2 prayer group and all the readers who gave substantial feedback and support, and anyone else who prayed and encouraged us along the way.

I also want to acknowledge all the brave men I have had the pleasure of working with over the years. My desire is that you walk in complete freedom all the days of your lives.

Especially, I would like to thank our children (and grandchild!) for their support along the way, from inception to the big push at the end of the project. Thank you, Daniel and Hampton (and Elizabeth) and Rees and Madison for reminding me that this is important and for adding value throughout the writing process. The Lord has told me to have the focus of a father/grandfather in my writing so that the message will be clearer. Thank you for being a focus for me.

And especially, *especially*, my wonderful and loving wife of thirty-two years, who has walked this *entire* journey with me. Kimberly, my bun, you have been, and continue to be, my greatest encourager and my favorite wise counselor. I love you dearly!

INTRODUCTION

Welcome! You are invited into a place of freedom from the control of pornography in your life. If you read no further in this book, I want you to know what is available to you in Jesus Christ and through this book. It may seem to those lost in pornography that this freedom is difficult, if not impossible, to attain. I understand that feeling. I am here to tell you that freedom is not only possible, it is within your grasp, so to speak.

John 8 is a profound chapter in the Bible. It starts with Jesus praying very early in the morning on the Mount of Olives, followed by a moment in the temple, where one of the most remarkable encounters ever witnessed takes place. It is while Jesus is teaching that the religious leaders of the day bring in a woman who has been caught in the act of adultery (for whatever reason, the man who has also been caught does not have to show his face) to force Jesus to take a side according to the Mosaic law, which requires this woman to be stoned for her sin.

They ask Him what He would do and, of course, His remarks throw them for a loop. Knowing that these religious leaders are simply trying to catch Him in an incorrect statement so that they can accuse Him and do away with Him, Jesus says, "He who is without sin among you, let him throw a stone at her first" (John 8:7 NKJV).

Of course, the religious tyrants slowly dispersed, leaving Jesus alone with the woman, whereupon He tells her that He also does not condemn her and for her to leave her life of sin behind. The woman, used as a pawn by the religious elite that day, left as a free woman. With the ending of this parenthesis in Jesus's morning He returns to teaching by stating, "I am the light of the world. He who follows Me shall not walk in darkness, but have the light of life" (John 8:12 NKJV).

This chapter continues Jesus's invitation to freedom, where He says things like, "If you abide in My word, you are My disciples indeed. And you shall know the truth, and the truth shall make you free" (John 8:31–32 NKJV) and "Therefore, if the Son makes you free, you shall be free indeed" (John 8:36 NKJV). The freedom that Jesus both shows and speaks of in John 8 is the same freedom available to you today. Even though our society, and even your own local culture, may have differing opinions on what may be "big" sins or "more embarrassing" sins, remember that sin is simply separation from God. Even though different sins may have different consequences, Jesus's invitation to freedom is available to all. To everyone. To you.

Whether young or old, if you have found yourself trapped in pornography, there is probably a very good chance that this book is not your first attempt at freeing yourself from its hold on you. You may have tried on multiple occasions to break the shackles of pornography use that have kept you bound. You may be afraid. You may doubt that freedom is even available to someone like yourself who has fallen as far as you know you have. You may also wonder why there continues to be a tiny glimmer of hope that raises its head every once in a while with the dream that you could ever have a life outside of pornography's bondage.

It's that glimmer of hope that Jesus referred to when He talked about the truth setting you free. You know this life in hiding is not living. Life in hiding can only be described as torment. Jesus has come that you may have life, abundant life (John 10:10). Jesus has a new life to bring to you that is not only out in the open but also filled with hope and a future (Jeremiah 29:11).

I spent years consumed by pornography in various forms. I understand that today access to pornography is very different altogether. Now you don't necessarily have to be glued to a large computer screen or a TV; access can come in the form of your phone, and access comes *AT* you just as much as you go after it.

As one who has found freedom in Jesus as it relates to pornography use, I want to take on the role of being your encourager, your cheerleader, so that you also will enjoy walking in all that the Lord has in store for you outside of this evil world.

This book is written from the context that freedom is available to you and may be closer than you might think or realize. I want you to know that you are not alone—even though I may never know you personally, I would like for you to know that I am here for you and that there are others supporting you as well. I have developed this freedom plan to be unapologetically simple. The challenge is not in the requirements but in the simplicity of following through. You can do this!

I have thoroughly enjoyed working alongside our son Rees, who is providing commentary from his life. As a recent college-graduate, he has provided me with significant insight on this topic from his age group and through his own experiences. I am confident that his additions will strengthen this discussion and cover some topics I have not.

Let me say it again: I invite you into a place of freedom from the control of pornography in your life. Today could be your day to grab hold of this freedom. Just as the woman caught in the very act of adultery started her day in sin and before lunch was a new person, you also may have witnessed your last scene of pornography, and today you really walk out from its hold over your life. Today can be your day!

Doug R. Conder, PhD

REES'S INTRODUCTION

Sexual sin and lust were viruses that nearly destroyed me, corroding my heart, mind, soul, and relationships in the process. I thought it would only find rest in the grave. I am learning that the Lord is the only thing that will satisfy me, the only thing that will fill the void in my soul, and the only true way for me to have complete victory in my sexual life. I found out about surrender. I had to quit making ultimatums or contracts and fall into the loving arms of my Father, who is willing to move heaven and earth for me to be free and to live a life of victory in my sexual life.

He wants me, and you, to succeed in this! The Lord wants us to live a life where we are an instrument that leads other men and women out of the camp of the enemy and into the camp of Life.

I really believe that my generation has the calling and the power to stand up against the complacent-mindedness that we have been fed—the belief that we are to struggle in this area of our life. The Lord has given us the power to rule over our bodies and the grace to control our desires. Are you ready to be free?

Rees J. Conder

CHAPTER 1

FROM FREEDOM
TO BONDAGE

THE CHILDREN OF Israel came to Egypt in Genesis 45 as the special guests of the strongest nation in the world. The Egyptian Pharaoh promised them the best, not only of the land (which was a primary pursuit of shepherds) but also of the food and produce of the country. While reconnecting with his father and brothers, Joseph was in a God-given position (Genesis 45:7–8 NKJV) to provide all that was needed to transport and settle the seventy family members from what was their home in Canaan to the breadbasket of Egypt.

Could it get any better for Israel? The family was back together, Joseph was second in command in Egypt, and his superior, Pharaoh, was more than happy to oblige whatever he requested for his family. Everything was looking up for Israel and his family.

In the background of this exciting relocation was the reality of a worldwide famine, and Joseph, the dreamer/ dream interpreter, had helped prepare the leadership of Egypt for the seven years of lack, which would affect the region and, in some cases, the globe. In Genesis 47:11 (NKJV), we are told of the final settling of Israel and their families in "the best of the land," and in verse 12, we see that Joseph "provided his father, his brothers, and all his father's household with bread." In the same breath, the scribe of Genesis states in the very next verse, "There was no bread in all the land; for the famine was very severe." It was during this moment that the famine began to bring about its harshest impact.

The story continues that the rank-and-file Egyptians and all the families of Canaan gave all their money to buy grain from Joseph, who oversaw the distribution of this all-important commodity. This, of course, brought about a failure of the monetary system. The next year of the famine, the people asked for grain by giving up any livestock that they might still own. So as the citizens brought their horses, flocks, cattle, and donkeys to

Joseph in exchange for grain, you can begin to see the downward spiral of the economy, with the government of Egypt now owning all relevant resources. All that was left was all that the people could offer the following year, which was their land and their own bodies as workers.

Over the course of a few years of famine, the political machine of Egypt owned the people, the land, the livestock, and all the financial resources. It was during this time the children of Israel had been provided for, and they comfortably multiplied exceedingly (Genesis 47:27 NKJV). Progress in the midst of desolation, excess in the midst of lack.

As the story transitions to the book of Exodus, we see in chapter 1 that the Israelites "were fruitful and increased abundantly, multiplied and grew exceedingly mighty; and the land was filled with them" (NKJV). At the same time, "there arose a new king over Egypt, *who did not know Joseph*" (NKJV; emphasis mine). As you would expect, the new Egyptian regime, operating out of fear, took captive the expanding population of the children of Israel as slaves, and made their lives miserable and terribly difficult. One day, they had grain and other food sources available at their beck and call, and a day later, they were being forced into a place of labor and hunger. What an abrupt shift in their lives and their idea of the future. They went from having it all to losing it all in the blink of an eye.

Many of us can relate to this feeling of having a world of plenty instantly followed by a crash of all that we hold dear. Similar to the children of Israel, many of us have landed in bondage, unexpectedly and without much notice. As if a rug had been pulled out from underneath us, we found ourselves on our backs with no immediate way to get to our feet. We begin to doubt that we can ever be free again.

Most of us have been in a place of protection and excess, and almost overnight, we found ourselves in bondage. Oh, we didn't believe we were trapped; as a matter of fact, we thought we were freer than ever before. We may not have noticed how our daily decisions and movements were slowly placing a noose around our own necks—and in those moments, we would've thought the noose was a necklace. There was a day, though, when you looked into the mirror of your soul and didn't recognize who you had become, what you had given yourself over to, and how far you were from home. It is at that moment that the battle truly begins.

This place of bondage may play out differently for each one of us, but don't be mistaken—it is bondage, and you are enslaved. For some, it is tied to the need for a substance—alcohol or another drug—while others may find it in financial battles that include gambling and the pursuit of the big payout. For many others, and myself, this enslavement is played out in pornography abuse and the sexual sin that surrounds this evil world. And yet to others, it may be control, manipulation, affairs (both sexual and emotional), theft, or the seemingly endless list of control-seeking mechanisms. No matter what the entanglement, our move from an Eden toward the Dead Sea occurs—for some quickly, almost overnight, and for others years in the making.

The Evil One works in unique ways, knowing what each individual has been susceptible to. For some, that means an immediate attack where, in a moment of time, someone finds themselves in a place that they never thought they would be, and they are instantly captured. For others, he approaches them by laying out months or years of smaller hooks, and they become immune to the barbs. Before they know it, hundreds of pricks have brought death from the multiple small wounds. He uses thousands of means to attack us, and no matter the method, we eventually become someone we cannot even recognize, doing things we never thought possible, not only to ourselves but also to the people we love.

Even amid this pain and anguish, even with the feelings of hopelessness and despair, we think back to a previous life where these pains were not an issue, and we pray for a way out. Some defer savoring these feelings of freedom by hiding deeper or running faster. Others recognize that they are trapped, irrevocably trapped, and give up hiding and running. Either way, we must be reminded that the Lord desires to draw us out with His cords of love and kindness.

Love. Kindness. Two things you never thought possible are fully available to you. The Lord also has a way for us to live outside of the hell in which we may have found ourselves, and that is what this book is all about.

To "change the course or direction of" is the definition of the word *redirect*. I am using this as the title of this book because those who have been lost in sin, especially the sin of pornography use, need a change of course. I encourage you to take advantage of the availability of a change *now*. If you're waiting for a perfect place to make a U-turn, it will not happen. The road you are heading down will potentially become narrower, and its shoulder will become more overgrown and harder to navigate.

Nevertheless, there are no lights on this road, and it is always dark. U-turns in those days will inevitably include deeper mud in the shoulder or even a drop-off cliff. These are not curses on your path, but the truth is that you need a redirect *now*. Please don't wait for a head-on collision before making your turn toward home.

CHAPTER 2

BONDAGE

WE SEE QUICKLY in Exodus 1 that the Israelites move from living in comfort to being trapped. Their lives are completely out of their control. All of us who have found ourselves buried in the garbage of pornography are also initially shocked. I'm assuming the Israelites felt this way as well. But for us, shame and the promises that "I will never do that again" begin to take over our personal narrative, and we are amazed and sickened all at the same time. A few people I know who have experienced this have shared with me their perspective on being lost, and I would like to share them with you, as a way of putting words to some of the feelings you may be experiencing.

The following word picture is a collage of comments by those who have been bound in pornography. I have compiled it into one description that puts feelings and experiences into words that may be beneficial in defining where you may have found yourself.

I've seen the cavelike sewer scenes in movies like *Les Misérables*, and I know this is a place I would never choose to go on my own. You can no doubt smell the sewer as you picture yourself stepping into the squishy ooze. I always viewed pornography as a sewer, one that I had no interest in stepping into ... until I did ... over and over again. Initially, the smell was shockingly poignant, making me sick to my stomach. Gradually, I found that I began to downplay the smell and the embarrassment of walking around in such a place. In a bizarre turn of events, I also found myself returning to the cave, wallowing in the filth, hiding out there, as I filled myself with visual images equivalent to the place where I was settling. While becoming accustomed to this wretched place, I found that I had also begun to feel somewhat at home, accepted, and even comfortable, feeling less shock and humiliation than before. I found myself setting up a home in the sewer—adding furniture, putting up pictures on the walls, and, in many ways, simply giving up. I felt that this was where I would live out my days as I learned to live the dual life of a sewer dweller and respectable member of society. It was at this time of my being an actor in a terrible drama that someone picked me out for the other life I was living, and my charade began to fall apart. I thought that this falling apart was to my detriment—and in many ways, it was—as I almost lost everything. In the end, being found out shone a light on this "home" I was dwelling in. My eyes saw it for what it was, and my nose smelled the stench of the sewer that I had called "my other life."

Have you ever felt like this? Have you ever felt that the cave you have moved in to is not the place in which you are meant to reside? If so, we will soon get to what I see are the solutions for living a full life free from the burdens and bondage of pornography.

Another quick picture for you, if I may. In our travels over the years, there have been opportunities for me to visit prisons in other countries to minister to those who are held captive for laws they have broken. First of all, I cannot imagine the depth of pain if you were sent for any period of time to a US prison. Overwhelming, I'm sure. In the prisons I have been to in India and Mozambique, I have seen single rooms that should hold about fifty prisoners, but instead, over a hundred would be stuffed into the room. Many of these prisoners are murderers and feel they have nothing more to lose by killing again. These rooms with cracked cinder block walls are dingy, terribly dark, and full of unimaginable smells; and the prisoners live there with little to no protection and even less hope. What we may see as a holding cell are where these prisoners sleep, eat, and live out their days and, even more fearfully, their nights.

I visited these prisons to try to bring hope to those who are imprisoned, to share how Jesus can take even the worst of us and make something new. The truth is that the prison these men live in is no worse than the prison any of us hidden in pornography lives in. Oh, we may think we live differently, with our large homes, full stomachs, and 600 thread-count sheets, but we are only delaying the inevitable truth that we are in a prison too.

My experience with pornography began as a surprise to me. Believe it or not, I had been protected from it for most of my early years, and it was not until I went to college that I was exposed to terrible pornographic movies in the dorm of my Christian university. I remember being a freshman walking down the hall of my dorm and noticing that one of the rooms had hacked the cable TV wires to access extra channels in their room. One of those channels would show graphic pornographic movies, and upon my first viewing, I knew I was trapped. I thought I was alone in this entrapment, as I would find my way to this room over and over, staying long after the room's inhabitants would leave to go to class or dinner. Years later, I now know that I was not the only one, but at that time, this secret life changed everything about me, and I felt so alone. So ashamed. So unworthy of His love. So guilty.

This marked a terrible turn, where I gave away years of my life to pornography's control. It was during this time that I felt isolated in my hidden world—at least I now know it was self-isolation, a part of my hiding in the sewer and considering this my new way of living ... and hiding.

Bondage is real, and in the midst of it all, I began to think that there was no other option because of what I had done and was doing, and having little to no hope of a life outside of this dark world. Have you ever felt this way?

Isn't it amazing the impact that pornography can have on a person's life? On *your* life! Isn't it amazing how you see things differently and operate from a place of hiddenness? How you know that you are lost but there seems to be no way out, so you stay around?

In the Community Bible Study's Ephesians study, it says, "Our minds can fixate on destructive ideas that we think will fulfill our desires. Instead, they only push us further away from the One who can satisfy our deepest longings" (Community Bible Study, 2023, p. 42). This clearly describes how this evil world takes hold of your soul, where you focus on the sewer world when life with Him is so near! You see, sexual sin engages a person physically, emotionally, and spiritually—all of us can get drawn away when we fall into this destructive world.

Unfortunately, what we allow ourselves to become enamored with has the immense power to bring us down. What are you infatuated with? What has a hold of you now? Conversely, we can also be full of hope, because what we become attached to can also have the power to save our soul!

I cannot begin to tell you how amazed I was that on the day I was writing about this life in bondage, the dictionary app I use posted their word of the day, and it was *duplicity*! This description of falling into bondage can be all-encompassing. You move from being singularly focused in word and in deed in every component of your life to being duplicitous, two-faced, and full of deception. That is a part of the destructive scenario of pornography.

Life as we know it is challenging enough with relationship issues, work demands, and daily problem-solving—right? But when we add the secret world of pornography into the mix, we bring on multiple challenges because what happens is that there are now two versions of you—the one that is public and the one that is private. Now you don't only have the prison of pornography to deal with, you also have a public life where you spend your time and energy trying to cover up your hidden life and deal with the challenge of living two lives with two competing masters.

Proverbs 11:3 (NIV) says, "The integrity of the upright guides them, but the unfaithful are destroyed by their duplicity." What happens within the bondage of pornography is that we try our best to make ourselves and others believe something that is *just* not true—that we are one person. In the inherent privacy of pornography use, we choose duplicity, and keeping both sides of who we are in play becomes increasingly difficult and virtually impossible.

Let me be even more clear here: You can't do it! The verse above tells you, in no uncertain terms, that you will be destroyed if you try duplicity. Of course, you may be thinking that you are the unicorn who can pull this off, and I would tell you, give up *now*. People more private and hidden than you could ever dream of have eventually crashed while trying to live two lives, and you eventually will too. Give up your keys to pursuing pornography and going down the highway of dual living, or the crash you will experience will be, to varying degrees, painful, public, and pervasive. There is a reason you try to keep your pornography use private. What is it?

Being trapped in bondage caused by our entanglement with pornography makes us see things differently, if not in a completely opposite light. The lies become truths, and the truths lies. The good and loving parts of your life become the distraction to the pursuit of filth and self-induced torment.

And *wow*, can this life change occur quickly! Even though we are all thrown a lifeline by a loving Father over and over, often through a loving human, we question whether or not we should grab it. Many disregard the rope thrown at them as they consider the waves crashing over their head more attractive than a dry cabin and a roaring fire. Others have little strength and even less hope that they can be among those snatched from the waves, and they let the rope slip through their grasp. And then there are the few, willing, simply willing, to reach for what seems to be the impossible chance of recovery, freedom, and life.

This book is written for those who are willing to die to their flesh and find a new way to live outside of pornography's control.

CHAPTER 3

FROM BONDAGE BACK
TO FREEDOM

THERE CAN BE both freedom and life as you learn to live outside of the bondage to pornography. As you have probably noticed, the focus of this book is not on the prevalence of pornography in our culture. Unfortunately, I'm assuming this as a given. My focus here is also not on the victims of the pornography industry even though I have a great deal of pain over the individuals who are trapped there. My heart hurts that these victims are entrapped simply because there is a demand.

In virtually every case, it is the men who have developed a depraved appetite for this evil that builds the demand that traps the victims. Without the enormous demand, the industry would implode. My desire is that the demand would shrivel up and the victims would be free simply because individuals stop consuming any amount of pornography.

The focus of this book is on those who have found themselves trapped in this evil world and seem to be stuck. Maybe you have little energy to break free and have found yourself falling deeper and deeper into the snare of pornography. Or maybe your desire is to live a life of freedom from the destruction of this evil world, and it hasn't occurred yet. Or maybe you have had some victories as it relates to pornography and you just need some support for your journey.

Whatever the stage of pornography consumption you may find yourself in, I want you to know that real freedom is available to you. I'm thoroughly convinced that with the steps I will outline in the remainder of this book, anyone and everyone can live a life of freedom. You will not only operate outside of the daily pursuit of this drug, but you will also live a life where your emotions are reignited, and your heart comes alive again. Through this healing, you will be able to love the Lord and others from a full heart of gratitude for what He has done for you (Romans 6 TPT).

In addition, I desire to see a noticeable shift generationally, especially in our young men, to rise above this entanglement and to walk in newness of life. I often think about the liar's ultimate pursuit through the evil mess of pornography and that is to destroy the family system that is God-assigned to bring life. All it takes are a few generations of men who are trapped in pornography who transfer this pain into their marriages and parenting for a culture to be lost.

I think it is quite apparent how quickly the impact of sexual sin has impacted our children and grandchildren. One of the biggest things many of us who work in this challenging mess see is how many young men seem to go down without a fight. Our culture portrays men as being hypersexualized, so many never even question when they find themselves fulfilling the curse that the culture has placed upon them. Just so we're clear here, I am not blaming the culture for something that is chosen. Many walk counter to cultural norms, and so can you.

The truth is that there is a way out. There is life to be experienced, there are marriages to be enjoyed, there are strong fathers to become, and there are the next generations of young men to support. My hope is that they will be equipped to fight this battle with confidence in Jesus Christ, knowing that there is success, life, and a beautiful future on the other side.

But it must begin *now*, and it must begin with *you*.

I dream of the day when, somehow, a generation of young men say "Yes" to being *that* generation that changes cultural history as we know it. Young men who rise up and pursue purity from a young age and join together to do so. Young men who take a public stand for Jesus Christ, which includes setting themselves apart as it relates to pornography and sexual sin. Young men who desire to grow up and father a second generation who would do the same. And so on and so on. This is where generations, one after another building on the Word of God and purity, have a chance to change our culture.

But it starts with one, and it starts with you.

The rest of this book is set up to assist you in developing a plan to experience freedom from pornography. Be aware that the pieces are easy to implement but more challenging to maintain. All are necessary for your freedom. Everyone's plan will look a bit different, but I am convinced that all of them must include all these pieces. Some of these pieces may seem easier to pursue than others, and I would dare to say the most challenging ones to you are probably the ones most important to your freedom. I am convinced that in each of the following segments, the level in which you engage in each area has a direct correlation with the pace of your recovery.

In other words, if you want to break free faster, you must delve deeper into each area. Choose to dive in and establish a plan for your freedom. If you are a young man, do this with your dad or a close friend. Do it in a men's small group. How about your dorm wing pursuing this as a group? Ask that your youth group leader start a group and do this together. Let me tell you, beyond a shadow of a doubt, your freedom is worth it. Jesus died for your freedom. Now buckle up and build your freedom plan.

So what is a freedom plan, and how are the pieces of this plan helpful? I'm glad you asked! For those trapped in any evil sin, there is the daily, if not hourly, anxiety of being so completely out of control. This is why when you're stuck in the hidden world of pornography, there is such a strong pursuit to hypercontrol every other area of your life, crying out for help because you are so completely out of control in the area of pornography use. You try to control your schedule, you try to control your media trail, you try to control everyone around you, you try to control *everything* to simply balance the area that is crushing your spirit that is So. Out. Of. Control. The antidote to being out of control is to find peace in a stable place. The freedom plan gives you the stability you need and a place to heal from.

The freedom plan is a list of vital components that, when fully implemented, bring life and peace to the individual. It is in this place that you can recognize your need for help and begin to operate with better decision-making skills and develop traction for living a full life. These components are all life-giving in nature and will increase your chances of attaining freedom. A full life is a life worth pursuing.

The freedom plan has been developed over the course of decades from both personal experience and that of hundreds of others I have had the pleasure to support along the way. The freedom plan does not necessarily involve steps that build upon one another but is, more simply, a blending of highest-priority healing and living components that are organically adjusting to meet your greatest need of the moment. This means that on any given day or week, the order or priority of this list could be completely realigned because the urgencies of your life at that moment call for different support mechanisms to be prioritized.

For example, as much as we would like for our lives to be systematized and orderly, it is not. Things happen day to day that require us to adjust our focus and address the needs of the moment. Receiving healing from the pursuit of pornography is the same; every moment has its own unique need. That is why we will look at these freedom plan components not as a series of steps to move through but as tremendous tools upon which we build a new life.

You will notice that the freedom plan is also never-ending. Every part of the plan involves strong and vital aspects of a full life and are items to build a good life upon. The characteristics of each of these components are also constantly changing to provide you what you need as you progress through various seasons of your life. Initially, I would encourage you to try to digest all the pieces together as each one will also help you in implementing the others.

Eventually, feel free to consider each of these components separately and return to the unique aspects at various seasons on your journey. Each component is important, but all together, all the components form a stable base on which to operate.

Lastly, the freedom plan is simply that—a plan to help you gain freedom from pornography use. Please don't worship the plan. Use it to help you see the Lord more clearly, because there is only true freedom in Him. I have based everything in the freedom plan on the scripture, but there is also a lot of scripture I've had to leave out because of space—I encourage you to go find more from the Word to build your freedom upon. Follow His lead, seek His face, find layers of freedom in Him, and live a full life.

Freedom Plan

- Repent/confess.
- Destroy the idols.
- Consume the Word.
- Pursue wholeheartedness.
- Serve the Lord, serve others.
- Develop a new life and daily schedule.
- Share your story.

CHAPTER 4

REPENT/CONFESS

THE FREEDOM PLAN that I will address in the remainder of this book consists more or less of suggestions for how to live your life in a new way far away from the world of pornography. What we find similar in all sin, and especially in pornography, is that we have broken trust with the Lord, and probably with others too. Repairing this trust should be your initial and primary pursuit. The feeling of being lost in sin is real. This is that feeling of *I am in over my head*, but not being convinced enough to truly announce this to anyone else. This is that *eyes-wide-open* moment where the fear of being found out consumes you.

In these moments, you either shut down emotionally

or hypercontrol the narrative of what's going on, and sometimes you actually try to do both at the same time out of being so terribly lost. As with any place where sin has overtaken us, we must repent of and confess our sins. These steps will begin to lift the covers over what has been hidden and is often your first substantial move toward home.

A quick aside for those who have not given their lives over to Jesus Christ: This will be the first step you will want to pursue. Trying to move forward in your own flesh will only be detrimental to your well-being, and very frustrating. Recognize that you are lost and in need of a Savior. I encourage you to connect with a Christian pastor to study the Bible and make this all-important decision first.

One necessary step for those coming out of bondage to pornography is to repent of this sin. Repentance is a "gracious invitation from a loving Father to come out of the tough places we put ourselves and find rest" (Kwan Porter, LifeMission Church Olathe, Kansas, January 22, 2023). As we step out of the shackles of pornography, there is a great possibility that there is a lot of sorrow, shame, and fear. It says in 2 Corinthians 7:10 (TPT), "God designed us to feel remorse over sin in order to produce repentance that leads to victory. This leaves us with no regrets." We see from this verse that repentance brings about victory. It also destroys any regret you may be feeling.

The challenge in all of this as it relates to pornography is the "remorse over sin" part. If there is no "remorse over sin," then you will not be in a position to repent of your sin and achieve victory. Many times, with pornography, when a person is caught in their sin, their remorse is less about a desire to change and more about how to respond to those who caught them. Until one experiences the God-designed feeling of remorse, the person is simply embarrassed for getting caught. It has been my experience that until there is remorse over our sin, there cannot be true repentance (which involves the changing of the mind and a turning away from something), and without repentance, there is a good chance you'll be right back where you were previously when the emotions you feel in the present die down.

In case you were wondering if you'll ever feel the full impact of remorse as it relates to pornography, you will. Whenever you see pornography the way the Lord sees it, you will experience a remorsefulness you will not soon forget. You will be broken knowing that only the

Lord can pick you up this time. This will lead you to full repentance or changing the way you think. When this happens, you will fully step away from pornography into a life of victory. There you will have no regrets!

In addition, repentance and a turning away from sin must become real through a life that is changed. John the Baptist says in Matthew 3 (NLT), "Prove by the way you live that you have repented of your sins and turned to God." What will that look like for you? Upon repentance, what will need to change to prove that you have repented of your sins? Besides your actions related to pornography, what else needs to change in how you treat others or in how you respond in certain situations? What a great opportunity to start over and change your life for the better!

Repentance is tied to the change in how you think about pornography and its impact on yourself and others. When you repent, you change your mind, and you see the sin through a different lens. It is the realization that your life has become a perverse lie. It is a crumbling over your sin and your perception of pornography. It is the recognition that you are dead in your sin and lost in your private world of filth and only the Lord can save you. Repentance is a turning away from your previous life toward a new way of living.

In addition, confessing the sin of pornography use is a vital step toward living in the fullness of what the Lord has in store for you. We are told in 1 John 1:9 (NKJV), "If we confess our sins, He is faithful and just to forgive us our sins and cleanse us from all unrighteousness." The confession of this hidden world is one of the most challenging steps you will undertake—and a necessary part of your being able to live in freedom and peace and being one with the Lord. Agree with God that you are lost in your sin, confess the sexual sins that you are guilty of, and ask for His forgiveness. Since He knows all things about our lives, there is no reason to hide or water down anything with Him. Upon your confession, you will receive the forgiveness available through Him.

The challenge of confessing sin in the area of pornography and other sexual sins is that there are often others involved who will be impacted by your confession. James 5:16 (NKJV) says, "Confess your trespasses to one another." It is my counsel that as you agree with God about your sin, you then confess this to someone that you can trust to help you walk this forward. A pastor, a mature believer, or a counselor are good people to consider. In addition, confess your sin to those closely associated with you who have been specifically impacted, including your parents, spouse, and others (of course, your age affects who these primary people might be). I personally think that you should consider having a pastor or a counselor as a part of your confession with those particular individuals who have been impacted, as they may potentially go through shock and a sense of betrayal themselves. Having others available during this time of confession will help everyone involved navigate their feelings and emotions.

I have attempted to lay out the importance of repenting of the sin of pornography use and confessing our sin to God, and to others too. Obviously, I see these as important to your walking in freedom, so why is this often a step that men want to jump past when it comes to pursuing purity and freedom?

Many times, I see guys wanting to do just about anything else to get freedom than these two foundational items. The reason I think this is the case is that *these are an acknowledgment of who you have been and a description of what you have done.* With that in mind, these can be two of the first truths you have encountered in a long time. That alone is new territory for someone leaving private sin.

To state that you are going to simply turn from something is one thing, especially when it is something that you have tried to turn from before without success. But turning from something evil (pornography) toward something beautiful (freedom) is worth the pursuit. Repentance, true repentance, is not a series of words without meaning, but the beginning of changing your mind regarding how you see the evil of pornography.

Confession, on the other hand, should not be seen as too difficult. Yes, I understand the fear of how you could be perceived when you confess the sin of pornography use and the uncertainty over how other people would respond. I also know that when coming out of difficult places to places of freedom, challenging conversations are necessary and worth it. This is why I personally think it is helpful for some confessions to take place in the presence of individuals who are committed to your healing as well as the healing of the relationships that may have been hurt by your actions. Anytime the truth comes forth, there is going to be progress.

I would really ask you to not consider moving forward to other aspects of your freedom plan apart from repenting of your sins and confessing your sins. The freedom plan, or any plan for that matter, will not work outside of repentance and confession. I call you, the men who are reading this book, to do the hard work necessary to position your mind and heart toward healing. Repent of your sins, confess your sins, and pray aloud this prayer (or something like it):

> *Jesus, I have believed a lie that there is life in any pursuit apart from You. I choose to turn away from pornography and ask that You change my mind in how I see it, that it is only evil and there is nothing of value in my association with it. I confess that I have thought* _____
>
> _____
>
> _____ *and done* _____
>
> _____ .
>
> *I ask that You forgive me of my sins. I want to return to You and love You with all my heart, soul, mind, and strength. I want to live with You as my only pursuit in life. Amen.*

FREEDOM PLAN:
REPENT/CONFESS

Contemplate: Set aside a period of time where you can, without interruption, process your life and experiences with pornography. Using pieces of paper or your phone, make a list of specific things you would like to turn away from as it relates to your pornography use. Be candidly clear and detailed about the things that you have found that have brought you the most pain and sorrow. Consider the things that you have tried so hard to hide, even from your own realization, and put those things on your list, as there is always something that needs to be brought to the light when you have invested so much in hiding it.

Answer: Have you repented or changed your mind about pornography? If so, what changes have you noticed in your thoughts? If not, what do you think is the wall that is holding you back?

Have you confessed to a trusted person what is really going on with your pornography use? If so, what was their response? If not, what is holding you back from doing this?

Pray: Lord, I need your help, again. I know that what I have read here is truth, and I need You to give me the courage to walk forward in this. Help me to see pornography the way You see it. Open my eyes to Your truth and help me to have Your heart. Beyond Your support, I ask, Lord, that you bring others around me to help. This is my time for freedom. Help me, Lord, in each next step. I love you, Jesus.

CHAPTER 5

DESTROY THE
IDOLS (PART 1)

FROM THE TEN Commandments in the Old Testament, of which the first is, "You shall have no other gods before Me" (Exodus 20:3 NKJV), to Jesus's statement in the New Testament that the first and greatest command is to "love the Lord your God with all your heart, with all your soul, with all your mind, and with all your strength" (Mark 12:30 NKJV), the Lord calls us to put Him first. Anything that we begin to adore or worship above Him has the potential of becoming an idol and should be dealt with accordingly.

Regardless of the reason you have found yourself immersed in pornography, you have found the pursuit to have a level of devotion connected to it, even from the very beginning. From your initial consideration of pornography to however far you may have gone, you have become devoted to it because you have given yourself over to it, to worship it, to give it control over you.

One of the primary steps in any freedom plan is to destroy both the idol and anything that supports it. What does that mean? The destruction of the idol of pornography is necessary to destroy the devotion one has developed to it. In addition, if the supports necessary to hold up an idol are gone, then the idol will topple over and crash to the ground on its own.

A simple word picture: If you had an antique crystal vase on the seat of an old wooden chair and you cut the four legs off the chair one leg at a time, the stability of the vase is compromised, right? Every leg that is cut off increases the chances of the vase falling. Even cutting off only one leg will have a significant effect on the chair's stability. The idol of pornography use is always supported or held up by a generous list of supports (the legs of the chair)—giving time to it in your schedule, increased comfort with duplicity, lots of lies, misuse of technology, ignoring old wounds, unhealthy privacy (hiding), and disengagement from relationships, along with many others.

The challenging yet rewarding decision to destroy the idols in your life to save your soul is 100 percent worth it. It's in the language of *destroying* that many bristle. You see, *idol maintenance is not idol destruction.* Those I have worked with who have tried to simply "do better" with their idol of pornography rarely get freedom from it. Those I have worked with who are willing to destroy the idol and its supports often get access to a new life of freedom and fullness in Jesus.

In addition, there is also a time element involved that we will see in every part of your freedom plan. The level you are willing to purge or destroy your idol is equal to the pace of your recovery. Let me give you some examples.

Lloyd is a single twenty-five-year-old young man who had a terrible and destructive relationship with pornography for most of his teens and twenties. He was only able to manage his pursuit of freedom because he was not willing to let anyone else know what was going on, and he also stated that he could not do away with his laptop and iPad because they were required for his work. The truth is that the "technology I need for work" excuse had less to do with his need for these items to do his work and more to do with his unwillingness to take the hard steps necessary to be free from pornography.

Johannes, on the other hand, was a newly married young man who carried a hidden world of pornography and chatroom abuse into his marriage. He was overwhelmed by his inability to break free when we discussed this important aspect of a freedom plan, including destroying one's idols. Whatever the reason for his readiness, whether it was his brokenness or just his weariness over the up-and-down nature of victories and defeats, he decided he was willing to destroy the idols. Johannes went all in, choosing to meet with a counselor alone and together with his wife for their marriage, as well as putting away his laptop that he had previously used for both work and his hidden life. In exchange, he set up an old desktop unit in their family room and used it for his workspace. He took the additional step of switching out his smart phone for a basic mobile phone, which did not have internet capability, as well as being vulnerable with his closest guy friends about what was going on with him personally and in his marriage.

I would hear from both Lloyd and Johannes individually every month or so, and I was shocked by the disparity of their results. Lloyd always wondered why things were not better—instead, they were actually worse—and why all his dating relationships ended soon after starting. Johannes had an eagerness, filled with hope, to tell of his victories and the things he was learning about himself. Purging the idols that bind us has an enormous impact on our souls and the level at which we purge does have an impact on the pace of our recovery.

I love the story of King Josiah found in both 2 Kings 22–23 and 2 Chronicles 34–35. The two generations prior to Josiah were evil, led by both his grandfather Manasseh and his father, Amon. With this spiritual history, Josiah did not grow up with an understanding of the law, which would have given him direction as to how to live; instead, he experienced the opposite. His grandfather built altars and placed carved images of various gods *in the temple* and was known for doing more evil deeds than the nations around them. Only in captivity at the end of his life did he turn to the Lord (2 Chronicles 33). His father built upon the heritage of evil so that Josiah had never seen the law of the Lord in practice in his younger years, and even in the early years of his reign as king, he did not know the Lord. It was not until he was sixteen years old that "he began to seek the God of his father David" (2 Chronicles 34:3 NKJV).

As a twenty-year-old, in his spiritual infancy, he began to purge all of Judah and Jerusalem of all the high places and the wooden, carved, and molded images. That's not all. He cut down the idols/images, broke them into pieces, and crushed them into powder. But wait, there's more. He exhumed and burned the bones of the priests on the altars before destroying the altars as well. It doesn't sound as though Josiah was willing to operate in his spiritual life alongside filth and ungodly practices. Josiah completely destroyed all the idols, altars, and images that the two previous generations had built.

No matter how much evil has been set up in your life, either by yourself or by the generations that preceded you, the only way forward, Josiah shows us, is through a complete reset and destroying, completely destroying what has been set up to destroy you.

I wish I could remember the date on the calendar when this happened, but I remember the day as if it was yesterday. Why I remember the day so well is because it was a day that changed everything for me.

It was my stake in the ground—not that I was perfect following this day, far from it, but every part of my growth following this was tied to this day.

It was a fifty-degree day, and I remember carrying our big Macintosh II computer, screen, and keyboard to a portion of land behind our house and spending hours destroying the "very expensive" computer with tree limbs, rocks, hoes, and my own strength. I remember picking up the screen (which in those days was not small) over my head and bashing it down on the rocks of the area, over and over again. I remember picking up thirty-pound rocks over my head and crashing them into the screen, over and over again.

I remember seeing and smelling what looked and smelled like sulfur powder floating out from the cracks in the screen. I remember not stopping even though an hour into this purging, I was gasping for a breath of air, sweat drenching my pants and sweatshirt. I remember screaming and yelling and going way beyond fatigue that day. This was the day I purged the idol that had dug its claws into my mind and heart.

And if there are any of you out there, operating from a current viewpoint, that I would just move to another computer I want you to know that this happened in the midst of my search for work, and that computer was my best source of leads. I didn't have an iPhone to seek work upon. If I had to look at a computer now, it would have to be at a public venue, and every minute on a screen cost us money we didn't have at the time.

But God...on that day, healing began, and I turned my life over to Him. I turned our marriage to Him, our family, and our future. The purging of the idol initiated something that could not have occurred without this first step. In a small way, I was taken into the Josiah story that day, hacking and beating, destroying and crushing, and pulverizing an idol that for too long had a part in telling me who I was. I left that holy plot of ground that day a new man—one who was sick of who I had become and ready to listen to how the Lord saw me. I was to be an *overcomer*. I was to be *victorious*. I was to be *free*.

The old lies began to fall off that day.

Maybe you need a stake-in-the-ground day yourself. Maybe you need to purge the idols that have controlled your heart and soul for too long. Maybe you need to be that Josiah, not only for yourself but also for those children and grandchildren who will walk in the wake of your legacy. Maybe, just maybe, today is the day you overcome the fear of the what-ifs in life and step into everything the Lord has in store for you.

WAKE UP!

Everything in creation mirrors the Lord. One of these is the general principal of our perception of light and darkness. In the natural, when we are close to a light, darkness beyond the area looks darker. Think also of an approaching thunderstorm, when you are standing in the sunlight. The approaching thunderstorm looks darker, and the light that you are in looks brighter too. *The closer to the light we are, the darker the darkness looks and feels.* In the natural, the longer we are in the dark, the better we adjust to it. We slowly become more complacent in this low-light setting, and we adapt to it. Spiritually, the same thing can occur. The longer we have been in darkness, the more we become comfortable with it. This sets one up for a big fall.

Are you tracking with me?

In order for us to break free from the bonds of sexual sin, we must be able to look into the darkness of the storm that is sexual sin, realize the filth that it truly is, understand how crippling and unfulfilling a life of sexual addiction is, and then fall into the loving arms of our Father of Lights. James 1:17 (TPT) says, "Every gift God freely gives us is good and perfect, streaming down from the Father of lights." When we can clearly see the darkness that is sexual sin, we will crave the Light more and more. When we clearly see the beauty of the Light of God, the darkness of sexual sin will look darker than it ever has before.

Prayer Point: Wake up! Ask God to reveal the degree of darkness that you may be walking in and pray to have a stronger desire for His Light.

CHAPTER 6

DESTROY THE
IDOLS (PART 2)

I PROMISE THAT all the parts of a freedom plan will not be broken into multiple parts; but with the destruction of idols, there's so much more for us to capture. I'm assuming that, as with many, this could be the most challenging step in your plan, and as I stated earlier, the most challenging steps toward your freedom are probably the most important ones. So, let's step forward in the Lord's strength, knowing that the purging of idols is a God thing, and because of that, it is of utmost importance to our freedom from pornography.

In Numbers 33, Moses tells the story of the journey

of the children of Israel from the point they left captivity in Egypt to their crossing of the Jordan River to take the land of Canaan. In this chapter, he finishes by initiating the conversation on the topic of dividing the land that they will soon take over; and how each tribe will settle into the land. Wrapping up in verse 55, Moses states (NKJV; emphasis mine), "But *if you do not* drive out the inhabitants of the land from before you, then it shall be that those whom you let remain *shall be irritants in your eyes and thorns in your sides, and they shall harass you in the land where you dwell.*" Let that sink in for a bit. No, really, let that sink in.

Moses knew that when the children of Israel entered the Promised Land, all its current inhabitants had to be completely destroyed so that the children of Israel could have a fresh start and a safe place to establish themselves with Yahweh. If they did not completely purge the land, the people, their gods, and their ways of living, all of it would negatively impact the children of Israel. They would be irritants and thorns to the Israelites, constantly harassing them. Moses knew that complete annihilation was necessary for this fresh start. This reminds me of our last chapter and Josiah's total pursuit of a complete purging of all the idols that could seemingly bring anguish and pain to the Israelites. There's a theme developing here.

I think it is even more poignant to notice that Moses says that failure to completely destroy them and their gods would bring about irritation to their eyes, a thorn in their side, and harassment by these inhabitants.

If we don't purge our own pornography-related idols, there will be irritation to our eyes and also in our hearts. Without purging our idols, there will be self-induced pain in our sides. Without purging our idols, we will be harassed, endlessly harassed, with shame and blame by the evil one who inhabits the land of pornography.

It is interesting to note that a generation later, Moses's assistant, Joshua, addresses the children of Israel at the end of his life regarding their claim on the land and its distribution to each tribe. He states in Joshua 23:11–13 (NKJV; emphasis mine),

> Therefore take careful heed to yourselves,
> that you love the Lord your God. *Or else*,
> if indeed, you do go back, and cling to
> the remnant of these nations—these that
> remain among you—and make marriages

with them, and go into them and they to you, know for certain that the Lord your God will no longer drive out these nations from before you. But *they shall be snares and traps to you, and scourges on your sides and thorns in your eyes,* until you perish from before this good land which the Lord your God has given you.

It's not surprising that Joshua would use some of the same language as Moses, as he was his assistant for many years. It is worth noting such similar responses to the Israelites not purging the land they were entering of its people and their idols. The impact of not destroying these people and their idols would come back to hurt the Israelites as a whipping to their sides, as a trap, and as thorns in their eyes. *If you don't completely destroy your idols, they can come back and cause you so much pain.* Think back to a time when you may have half-heartedly left pornography behind. What came back to you? Your experience was not freedom, was it? Rather, it was a boomerang effect that was more devastating than your original struggle. These were the things Moses and Joshua were trying to prevent. Destroying the idols that you have worshipped is meant to help prevent the same things from happening to you over and over.

To add one more layer to this, it is interesting to take note of Joshua 10:28–11:23 (NKJV), which describes the actual conquest of the land, with multiple depictions of the Israelites taking over the land. The consistent language being used cannot be overlooked as it is a guide for us as we purge our own idols/enemies. At least eight times it describes their conquest as "utterly destroying" the enemy; at least ten times it states, "they let none remain," or "left none breathing," as well as a few "they struck all the people with the edge of the sword."

This language gives us a picture of what our pursuit of our own promised land will look like and what it will take to accomplish it. These phrases are ones that don't allow for the survival of something. Maybe you need to adjust your language to adjust your heart—instead of *managing* your pornography use, you should be utterly *destroying* it. Other words for destruction you may want to consider adding to your vocabulary relating to the pursuit of your freedom are *annihilate, demolish, exterminate, obliterate,* or *eradicate.* How you define your pursuit of freedom will have a significant role in how you actually carry it out.

At a time when you are entering a new land of freedom, I hope that we can learn from these examples how important it is to completely destroy what could get in our way to complete freedom. It's difficult enough to try to be free when bound by past chains that we allow to hold us back. Allowing past idols to linger will only slow down our freedom progress, and for some, it will stop it altogether. My experience has taught me that you have the greatest chance of living in freedom if you destroy, completely and utterly destroy, any and all idols that have kept you bound.

FREEDOM PLAN:
DESTROY THE IDOLS

Contemplate: Take ten to fifteen minutes to quietly consider how pornography is an idol for you. Look into your soul and determine how you see it, miss it, handle it, and, possibly, how you protect it. How would you define pornography's role in your life, and how does that response factor into whether or not it is an idol for you? Take the time to evaluate your schedule and your level of desire for pornography and give it a definite title. Is it an idol?

Answer: We all have certain friends that we go to first when we are in need. If pornography were to be classified as a "friend" of yours, how quickly do you go to it when you are stressed or in a "situation"?

What are the idols you would like to destroy? Be very specific. Pornography is a category. Be specific about what your idols are.

What are the corresponding supports that have kept these idols alive and active? What supports, if taken away, would cause your idols to fall?

What have been your excuses for not destroying either the idols or their supports?

Be real: How much time in a week have you given over to pornography in all its various forms?

What does destruction look like for the idols/supports you have listed?

Who else knows about your idols? Who do you trust to share this with? Go over your answers to these questions with that person and ask them to help you.

Pray: Father, my worship has not been dedicated to You. I have given myself over to another, and it is destroying my life. Please be near to me now and help me to see things the way You see them. Help me to see pornography and my setting it on a hidden precipice for what it is. I am in great need, Lord. I open my heart to You now and ask You to take over.

New Day

We have all experienced it before—the sickening feeling of having fallen into sexual sin, yet again. The words of Paul in Romans 8 (NIV)— "Therefore, there is now no condemnation for those who are in Christ Jesus"—rarely seem possible, or even real, at this low point. A personal pitfall for me has been the belief of simply having "good" days and "bad" days. "Good" days were days of victory, while "bad" days were days when I fell into sexual sin or lust at some point in the day.

The obvious problem with this mindset is that if you stumble into sexual sin in the morning, then you begin to think, *What's the point of trying to fight* if the feelings of temptation come back later in the day? This false belief held me captive for way too long. If God is worthy of every day, then He is certainly worthy of every hour, minute, and second that we can give Him.

When the Lord says that he washes our sins white as snow (Isaiah 1:18) and that as soon as we repent, He takes our sins as far as the east is from the west (Psalm 103:12), He means it. When we cry out to the Lord in surrender, He forgives us at that exact moment. A *new day* can begin at any point in the day. These are some of the hardest battles we will face (saying no to something we allowed ourselves to indulge in even minutes earlier), but victories in these battles always carry the most weight. Win the battle, and you will eventually win the war!

CHAPTER 7

CONSUME THE WORD

ANOTHER KEY COMPONENT to any freedom plan is filling yourself with the Word of God, the Bible. In many cases, when someone stumbles into and begins to dwell in the land of pornography use, they give themselves over to a time-consuming pursuit. When busy people who have full schedules (that's all of us) become entwined in pornography, it's amazing how you find time or make time for this evil world. Whether you watch it late at night or you choose to finish tasks quicker to return to pornography, it's amazing how much time you can find for this sinful venture.

Oftentimes, the areas where this time is scavenged from are our most beneficial and useful periods—quiet time with the Lord, prayer, reading the Word, Bible study, time with your spouse and family, church activities, or even exercise. In most cases, the good things that we throw away to spend our time with pornography are exactly the things that would give us the perspective and wise counsel we need to release ourselves from its evil clutches. This is why one of the vital pieces of a freedom plan is the re-prioritizing of the nourishment necessary to live as a free man. Digging into the Word and spending time in prayerful meditation play a role in our coming to freedom. They become even more important in our endeavor to stay in freedom. Or, as the Lord shared with me one day, "Devour the Word or be devoured by the world."

Let's return to the story of Josiah, as there is a completely different component of this story that is so vital for us to catch. When Josiah was twenty-six years old—he had been in power as king for eighteen years now—he sent his scribe, governor, high priest, and other officials to oversee the repairs to the temple from all the years of its use housing the idols, images, altars, and the evil practices of the previous generations. In the midst of this construction zone, Hilkiah, the high priest, made an earth-shattering discovery. Somewhere under all the dust and piles of stone and timber, with hundreds of craftsmen skillfully restoring the temple, the high priest finds the Book of the Law of the Lord given to Moses in the house of the Lord.

Let's not lose sight of what just occurred in our Josiah story: The high priest has just found the Book of the Law of The Lord in the temple! Does that seem like an odd discovery to you? Where else would you think you would find the Book of the Law except in the temple? How interesting was it that the high priest, and not one of the other officials, found the Book of the Law in the temple? Or how about this: How was the Book of the Law lost in the first place? Read that last question again and let it settle in your soul.

You see, *when the Word was lost, the people were lost.*

For at least two generations, evil practices were carried out in the temple, which was established to worship Yahweh, the only true God. And there, amid the temple, which was being restored, sat the Book of the Law. Two quick points here: First, without the Word, the people were left to their own evil devices, and two generations were lost. Second, in the midst of your temple being restored from the impact of the idol worship of pornography, there is a Word available to you, and it has often been right under your nose.

Just as these two generations' lack of access to the Word opened the floodgates of evil, I would think that there has been a distance, if not a complete separation, of your being in the Word while lost in your pornography nightmare. The time-eating world of pornography takes us away from the many areas in our lives where time is needed to develop character and strength. We need time to consume the Word of God. When we step out of pornography use, redirecting that-now available time toward our growth is doubly beneficial.

So what does consuming the Word look like? That's a great question! What I recommend initially as you break free of pornography is to partake of large swaths of scripture at a time, for two reasons: One, it gets you used to transferring large chunks of time from something deadly to something that is life-giving. Two, you're malnourished and need to start fueling your soul again. What you will begin to notice as you do this is that the brokenness you are coming out from gives you a context in which to digest the Word in a whole new way.

For example, as you read large sections of scripture,

your eyes and soul will read the Word from your place of pain, and the Lord will begin to minister to you. Don't get too caught up in what books and chapters you are reading as the Lord has the capacity to use any part of the Bible to work on you. Much of this freedom plan is growing out of an obscure passage of scripture about an Old Testament boy-king that when read by most people appears to be only a historical narrative of one of those many kings in the Old Testament. But to me, and I hope to you as well, it is the story of breaking out and being free and the steps to make that happen. Consume the Word, as it is your source of life.

Clark, a single young man who approached me about his ongoing struggle with pornography, took this part of the freedom plan very seriously. With the pain of having to come to grips with how lost he had become, he chose to go all in, in the area of consuming the Word. He knew that this area of his life had become dull, and he had really just stopped reading the Bible, so he chose to try to reignite his soul by immersing himself in the Word. How he did this was unique to him, just as all of us will have to find our unique way of making life changes to combat pornography's control.

During his days and nights in the clutches of

pornography, Clark found himself acting as though he had no control over his time—any moment when the urge to delve into pornography emerged, Clark would give in, seemingly without any fight at all. In response to this, Clark chose to give his nights and days to reading and absorbing the Word. By choice, he would wake up two hours earlier than he was used to and, with a cup of hot coffee, read the Word out loud over himself. He chose to divide his lunch hour: he would eat quickly for the first thirty minutes and then read the Bible for the last thirty. During this season of time, Clark chose to forgo other forms of entertainment at night, so no movies, no binge-watching a TV series, or aimless surfing on the internet. This opened his night to at least another two hours of reading time, as well as gave him time to join a men's small group at his church, where they openly discussed the topic of pornography use and the benefits of living a life that is free of its hold.

What is so interesting to note about Clark's example is that he initially set out to do this for two weeks to jump-start his heart. Two months into this new life in the Word, Clark stated that this new schedule had grown on him, that he noticed a significant change in his heart, and his desire for pornography had also substantially diminished. Clark also stated that he was sleeping better, even though he had fewer sleeping hours with the early wake-up. He also acknowledged that he felt that he had more time in his day even though he was spending over four hours reading the Bible!! Extreme example? Maybe for some, but not for those who know the feeling of being so lost they are willing to do just about anything to break free.

Before we move forward, let me address a major topic as it relates to consuming the Word—the likelihood that you may not be interested in reading what the Word has to say, or you're convinced that you just can't find the time. As you have dunked yourself in the pit of pornography, you have begun to believe the lie that the Word, the church, and seriously following Jesus isn't a part of the answer to your problems. Let me tell you straight up: separating yourself from these things is what has gotten you here in the first place. Ephesians 4:19 (TPT) says, "Because of spiritual apathy, they surrender their lives to lewdness, impurity, and sexual obsession."

Let me break this down for you: The spiritual apathy mentioned in this verse means a lack of feeling, emotion, or concern; and the verse states that the result of this is the evil and wickedness that comes with impurity and being obsessed with sexual pursuits. One of the primary synonyms of *lewd* is *pornographic*! So being in a place where you are disinterested in or indifferent to spiritual matters or you just don't see it as a priority, opens the door to surrendering yourself to the destructive underworld of pornography.

It is extremely important that we see this indifference to spiritual things for what it is. Your apathy toward the things that are your only hope is as silly as saying that you're choosing to keep all the doors of your house propped open all day while you're at work and expecting all your belongings to stay safe. If spiritual apathy then opens the door to pornography and all sexual perversion, then the opposite is indeed true.

Filling yourself with the Word closes the door to evil and strengthens you to endure and stand firm. It's very interesting to note that Paul says later in Ephesians to take up the sword of the Spirit, which is the Word of God, as the only offensive weapon we have to fight against evil. This link that Paul ties together for us is that *spiritual apathy brings about sexual obsession and is remedied with the sword of the Spirit, the Word of God.* If you have been indifferent to spiritual things, let me encourage you to repent of being unconcerned or disinterested in them because you now see the result of where this spiritual apathy can take you.

Large sections of scripture from a place of desire will fill you up, and yes, you are starving for the Word. I find it interesting that there are all these eating metaphors in the past few paragraphs (maybe it's dinnertime!), until I noticed that this part of your freedom plan is so important because you need a new diet for a new you! The diet of filth and wasted time has virtually killed you, and you must learn to get good food in your soul so you can heal and be restored. Consuming the Word accomplishes this.

Many of us need to find a new way to read the Word. Maybe you're not a traditional reader, or you're very busy. Be creative in how you get the Word into you—audio Bible, giving up your lunch time for the Word, reading out loud in your home over your wife and children, memorizing and quoting important verses, etc. *Remember: You creatively found time for pornography—why not use your creativity to find the best way to consume the Word?*

Be aware that you need to recover from your malnourishment with high-calorie sections of the

Word—chapters and chapters, books and books, because remember, you have large chunks of time that you are transferring from darkness to light, and you're fueling an empty soul. After months and months of consuming the Word, you will begin to feel more settled, and at this point, you might find the ability and the focus to study specific smaller sections of scripture. It is at this point that you may benefit from a targeted study guide or a class to pour your time into.

Of course, in the midst of my encouraging the pursuit of massive quantities of the Word, please do not lose sight of some of the small individual verses—those that when taken to memory become daily reminders to live by. I am including some of these at the end of the chapter as a small plate for you to start your larger meals from.

I love that the living Word of God is "full of energy, like a two-mouthed sword. It will even penetrate to the very core of our being were soul and spirit, bone and marrow meet! It interprets and reveals the true thoughts and secret motives of our hearts. There is not one person who can hide their thoughts from God, for nothing that we do remains a secret, and nothing created is concealed, but everything is exposed and defenseless before His eyes, to whom we must render an account" (Hebrews 4:12–13 TPT).

I have experienced multiple seasons in my life where the consumption of the Word has filled my days and many of my nights. During the many hours of reading, I have found ministry and direction breaking forth in my lost life. I can't begin to tell you how many times in the course of my reading, and in the many times when I read *way* out loud for hours on end, the Lord has addressed things in my heart—(He even penetrates to the very core of our being where soul and spirit, bone and marrow meet) or given me counsel regarding a particular work or family situation. The Word opens the door for understanding, but for those who are stepping up out of the sewer of pornography, it provides healing, and that is why we need a lot of the Word because we need a lot of healing. The Word is an ointment that soothes. The Word is a path to the Light. The Word is the restorer of our broken souls.

Before we wrap up this chapter, I would like to offer another aspect of consuming the Word, and that is allowing the spoken Word of God to claim who we are in Him. What I mean by this is the Word of God has the power to overwhelm all spirits of darkness, and it prevails over all the demons that you have given yourself over to during your bondage in pornography. Much of scripture is declarative in nature and is perfect to be read in a manner where you bring the truth of scripture into the situation in which you now reside. In other words, if you don't have your own language to define who you now are, use the words of the Bible as personal declarations of who you desire to be. Reading the Bible out loud and integrating yourself into the words of scripture is *powerful*!

For example, in Romans 12 the first two verses could be read as "By the mercies of God, I present my body a living sacrifice, holy, acceptable to God, which is my reasonable service. And I will not be conformed to this world, but be transformed by the renewing of my mind, that I may prove what is that good and acceptable and perfect will of God." Try reading this slowly and out loud over yourself several times a day.

Another is found in Colossians chapter 3:1–5, where you can read, "I have been raised with Christ, I seek those things which are above, where Christ is, sitting at the right hand of God. I set my mind on things above, not on things on the earth. For I have died, and my life is hidden with Christ in God. When Christ who is my life appears, then I also will appear with Him in glory. Therefore, I put to death the members which are on this earth: fornication, uncleanness, passion, evil desire, and covetousness, which is idolatry." Again, read and declare this over yourself as often as you can.

One more thing before we close this chapter: You will need to break any agreements you have made with pornography so that you don't take them into your new life. What have you agreed to as it relates to your use of pornography? Have you believed that pornography is your "escape" or your "private world"? Have you thought at any point in time that you deserve this time for yourself? Have you seen pornography use as "not that big of a deal"? Have you ever rationalized that your pursuit of pornography is "not as graphic or as consuming as others" and thus is not as offensive? Have you blamed others and not taken responsibility for your own choices? Whatever your agreements—in reality, all your agreements are lies—it is imperative that you break those agreements. The Lord will bring those agreements to mind when you pray, and you can then break your constant agreement with those lies. Sometimes the agreements are simply the thoughts you have used to explain away the severity of your life in pornography.

Pray something like this:

> *Lord, Jesus, I come under Your refuge and ask You, Spirit of Truth, to reveal to me any agreements I have made related to my use of pornography. Holy Spirit, please show me what agreements I have made with the enemy, what lies I have believed? (Be still and listen ... and write down what you hear). I ask You, Lord, to expose all lies, shine Your light into any aspects of darkness hidden in me (Be still and listen ... and write down what you hear). I break these agreements in the authority of Jesus Christ. I renounce these lies that I have believed and operated from and ask You, Lord, to wash me now in the blood of Jesus. I separate myself from these past agreements now in Jesus's name and say that I will not operate from these lies again. Thank You for healing me and transforming me, Lord. Amen.*

Lastly, you will find it incredibly valuable to take back ground in the Spirit and take authority over the buildings, rooms, computers, phones, etc., that you may have handed over to evil. This can be done by consecrating and cleaning all technology with the blood of Jesus. John Eldredge (*Wild at Heart* newsletter, May 2023) provides a great example of this when he wrote this declaration, which can be read over your home and work locations: "I bring all computers, tablets, cell phones, apps, television, and cable in our home under the rule of the Lord Jesus Christ. I cleanse all technology in this house with the blood of Christ, including all internet, Wi-Fi, cellular signals, and all cable and media. I command the blood of Christ and the Glory of God to filter all media, signals, and internet coming into our homes, including through our cell phones. In the name of the Lord Jesus."

Your freedom plan must include the benefits that come from diving deep into the Word of God. This is not a box to check but an innate need for all humans, especially those who are breaking free from anything that has negatively controlled them. Consuming the Word is not a destination but an invitation to join in what He wants to do *in* you. As you add this to your freedom plan, I am confident that you will never be the same. Bless you as you dive in.

FREEDOM PLAN:
CONSUME THE WORD

Appetizer scriptures: Choose three to five of the scriptures below and do the following:

1. Commit them to memory.
2. Write them out by hand ten times a day.
3. Read them into your voice memos on your phone and play them four to five times a day.
4. Journal a paragraph using a different verse each day as a jumping-off spot.
5. Text a verse to someone else to encourage them.

Psalm 16:1, 16:11 (NKJV)

> Preserve me, O God, for in You I put my
> trust. ... You will show me the path of life;
> In Your presence is fullness of joy; At Your
> right hand are pleasures forevermore.

Psalm 18:1–3 (NKJV)

I will love You, O Lord, my strength. The
Lord is my rock and my fortress and my
deliverer; My God, my strength, in whom
I will trust; My shield and the horn of my
salvation, my stronghold. I will call upon
the Lord, who is worthy to be praised; So
shall I be saved from my enemies.

Psalm 27:1 (NKJV)

The Lord is my light and my salvation;
Whom shall I fear? The Lord is the
strength of my life; Of whom shall I be
afraid?

Psalm 101:3–4 (NKJV)

I will set nothing wicked before my eyes;
I hate the work of those who fall away;
It shall not cling to me. A perverse heart
shall depart from me;
I will not know wickedness.

Psalm 119:9–11 (NKJV)

> How can a young man cleanse his way?
> By taking heed according to Your word.
> With my whole heart I have sought You;
> Oh, let me not wander from Your commandments!
> Your word I have hidden in my heart,
> That I might not sin against You.

Proverbs 10:9 (NKJV)

> He who walks with integrity walks securely, But he who perverts his ways will become known.

Proverbs 11:3 (NIV)

> The integrity of the upright guides them, but the unfaithful are destroyed by their duplicity.

Mark 12:28–31 (NKJV)

> Then one of the scribes came, and having heard them reasoning together, perceiving

that He had answered them well, asked Him, "Which is the first commandment of all?"

Jesus answered him, "The first of all the commandments is: 'Hear, O Israel, the Lord our God, the Lord is one. And you shall love the Lord your God with all your heart, with all your soul, with all your mind, and with all your strength.' This is the first commandment. And the second, like it, is this: 'You shall love your neighbor as yourself.' There is no other commandment greater than these."

John 8:31–32 (NKJV)

Then Jesus said to those Jews who believed Him, "If you abide in My word, you are My disciples indeed. And you shall know the truth, and the truth shall make you free."

John 8:36 (NKJV)

Therefore if the Son makes you free, you shall be free indeed.

John 10:10 (NKJV)

> The thief does not come except to steal, and to kill, and to destroy. I have come that they may have life, and that they may have it more abundantly.

Romans 8:5–6 (NKJV)

> For those who live according to the flesh set their minds on the things of the flesh, but those who live according to the Spirit, the things of the Spirit. For to be carnally minded is death, but to be spiritually minded is life and peace.

Romans 12:1–2 (NKJV)

> I beseech you therefore, brethren, by the mercies of God, that you present your bodies a living sacrifice, holy, acceptable to God, which is your reasonable service. And do not be conformed to this world, but be transformed by the renewing of your mind, that you may prove what is

that good and acceptable and perfect will of God.

Romans 12:9 (NKJV)

Let love be without hypocrisy. Abhor what is evil. Cling to what is good.

Romans 15:13 (NKJV)

Now may the God of hope fill you with all joy and peace in believing, that you may abound in hope by the power of the Holy Spirit.

1 Corinthians 6:13 (NKJV)

Now the body is not for sexual immorality but for the Lord, and the Lord for the body.

1 Corinthians 6:20 (NKJV)

For you were bought at a price; therefore glorify God in your body and in your spirit, which are God's.

1 Corinthians 10:21 (NKJV)

> You cannot drink the cup of the Lord and the cup of demons; you cannot partake of the Lord's table and of the table of demons.

1 Corinthians 13:11 (NKJV)

> When I was a child, I spoke as a child, I understood as a child, I thought as a child; but when I became a man, I put away childish things.

2 Corinthians 5:17 (NKJV)

> Therefore, if anyone is in Christ, he is a new creation; old things have passed away; behold, all things have become new.

2 Corinthians 7:10 (NKJV)

> For godly sorrow produces repentance leading to salvation, not to be regretted; but the sorrow of the world produces death.

Galatians 5:16–17 (NKJV)

> I say then: Walk in the Spirit, and you shall not fulfill the lust of the flesh. For the flesh lusts against the Spirit, and the Spirit against the flesh; and these are contrary to one another, so that you do not do the things that you wish.

Galatians 6:7–9 (NKJV)

> Do not be deceived, God is not mocked; for whatever a man sows, that he will also reap. For he who sows to his flesh will of the flesh reap corruption, but he who sows to the Spirit will of the Spirit reap everlasting life. And let us not grow weary while doing good, for in due season we shall reap if we do not lose heart.

Ephesians 2:1–10 (NKJV)

> And you He made alive, who were dead in trespasses and sins, in which you once walked according to the course of this world, according to the prince of the

power of the air, the spirit who now works in the sons of disobedience, among whom also we all once conducted ourselves in the lusts of our flesh, fulfilling the desires of the flesh and of the mind, and were by nature children of wrath, just as the others.

But God, who is rich in mercy, because of His great love with which He loved us, even when we were dead in trespasses, made us alive together with Christ (by grace you have been saved), and raised us up together, and made us sit together in the heavenly places in Christ Jesus, that in the ages to come He might show the exceeding riches of His grace in His kindness toward us in Christ Jesus. For by grace you have been saved through faith, and that not of yourselves; it is the gift of God, not of works, lest anyone should boast. For we are His workmanship, created in Christ Jesus for good works, which God prepared beforehand that we should walk in them.

Ephesians 4:19 (TPT)

Because of spiritual apathy, they surrender their lives to lewdness, impurity, and sexual obsession.

Philippians 3:12–14 (NKJV)

Not that I have already attained, or am already perfected; but I press on, that I may lay hold of that for which Christ Jesus has also laid hold of me. Brethren, I do not count myself to have apprehended; but one thing I do, forgetting those things which are behind and reaching forward to those things which are ahead, I press toward the goal for the prize of the upward call of God in Christ Jesus.

Colossians 3:1–3 (NKJV)

If then you were raised with Christ, seek those things which are above, where

Christ is, sitting at the right hand of God. Set your mind on things above, not on things on the earth. For you died, and your life is hidden with Christ in God.

James 4:7–10 (NKJV)

Therefore submit to God. Resist the devil and he will flee from you. Draw near to God and He will draw near to you. Cleanse your hands, you sinners; and purify your hearts, you double-minded. Lament and mourn and weep! Let your laughter be turned to mourning and your joy to gloom. Humble yourselves in the sight of the Lord, and He will lift you up.

1 Peter 4:1–2 (NKJV)

Therefore, since Christ suffered for us in the flesh, arm yourselves also with the same mind, for he who has suffered in the flesh has ceased from sin, that he no longer should live the rest of his time in the flesh for the lusts of men, but for the will of God.

1 John 2:15–17 (NKJV)

Do not love the world or the things in the world. If anyone loves the world, the love of the Father is not in him. For all that is in the world—the lust of the flesh, the lust of the eyes, and the pride of life—is not of the Father but is of the world. And the world is passing away, and the lust of it; but he who does the will of God abides forever.

1 John 5:11–12 (NKJV)

And this is the testimony: that God has given us eternal life, and this life is in His Son. He who has the Son has life; he who does not have the Son of God does not have life.

CHAPTER 8

PURSUE
WHOLEHEARTEDNESS

AS YOU STEP out of the pit of pornography, you may be asking yourself the question, "Who am I?" Oftentimes, when you have placed your time, energy, and devotion into anything, it can begin to define who you are. Let me remind you: From the very start, you have been bought with the precious blood of Jesus. When you give yourself over to Him, you are labeled as one of His, a Christian, a child of God.

No one else, especially the demon Satan, has a credible voice in telling you who you are. Remember, when he lies, he speaks his native language (John 8:44 NIV). All he knows is lies. Answering the question of who you are is part of you being seen as a new creation, where the "old things have passed away; behold, all things have become new" (2 Corinthians 5:17 NKJV).

As you continue to move forward in establishing and following a freedom plan it is imperative that you position yourself in Him and engage in the redefining power that comes from being in Christ. A necessary part of being in Christ is your choice of who you worship. During your life of bondage to pornography, it would have been difficult for an outsider looking in to say that you were worshiping anything but yourself and your own selfish desires. Seeing yourself for who you formally were is necessary as you look to become His, fully His.

I want to be a simple guy as it relates to following Jesus. My pursuit is to do the things that He says are important and not get distracted by too many opinions and thoughts of man. Jesus was overtly clear that if there was only one command it would be to "love the Lord your God with all your heart, with all your soul, with all your mind, and with all your strength. This is the first commandment" (Mark 12:30 NKJV). This profound statement Jesus made to the religious scholars of His day is just as profound and thoroughly directive to us today. He wants all of us. Trying to do it any other way, less than being all in, is setting yourself up for disappointment. He has a plan for your life, and it requires all of you to make it happen.

One of the biggest challenges for men leaving pornography behind is that they really aren't willing to leave pornography behind. They still want to dabble.

What do I mean by dabble? Dictionaries give a lot of great definitions, but I don't think they hit the mark completely on this one. I see dabbling as not being all in on something or being wishy-washy or apathetic about your pursuit of something. If you're dabbling about being on a diet, then chances are you're not going to lose a lot of weight. If you dabble with exercising, you shouldn't really expect to get cut or chiseled any day soon. *You won't survive dabbling with pornography*—it's like stepping into a small child's sandbox with ten twelve-foot adult king cobras and thinking it's playtime. So, if there's no such thing as dabbling with pornography, then why do I find this so often to be the case for someone who wants to step away from pornography? It's because we don't fully know what we're dealing with! The evil of pornography will not leave you alone. You must desert it completely and fill that space it occupied in your life with something much more valuable.

If I've had this conversation with one man, I've had it with hundreds. I ask them something like, "On a scale of 0 to 100 percent, how willing are you to leave your hidden world of pornography?" You know the answer I get, right? It's always "One hundred percent." Then why does almost every man end up in their willingness scale at something around 70 percent? It's simply that their desire for 100 percent doesn't consider how truly difficult it is to leave any hidden world, especially that of pornography.

It has been my experience, both personally and from working with hundreds of men, that there is only one way to be free from pornography, and that is to be completely given over to something greater. It says in 2 Peter 2:19 (NIV), "People are slaves to whatever has mastered them." In most cases, the cruel taskmaster of pornography is broken only when you give yourself over to a greater Master.

One of my favorite verses in the Bible is Psalm 119:9–11. Of course, I love this verse, not only because of what it says but, more importantly, also because of how clearly it lays out this primary component of your freedom plan. There is no other way to interpret this verse, and it is almost always the first verse I study with someone who wants to break free from pornography. Either you accept this verse for what it says and pursue this, or you must choose to neglect it. These verses don't allow for a middle ground. As I have said before, every aspect of a freedom plan can be challenging, but the component of your wholehearted pursuit of the Lord, as challenging as it may be, could also be one of the most rewarding ones to capture.

Psalm 119:9–11 (NKJV, easily remembered by 119:911) gives a clear answer to the question asked in the first line: "How can a young man cleanse his way?" Or how about the same question from The Passion Translation: "How can a young man stay pure?" This is the core question we must answer as we consider a life outside of pornography use. Reading a clear answer to this foundational question is the easy part; doing it is the challenge.

In the New King James Version, the answer to the question of the first line goes like this: "By taking heed according to Your Word. With my whole heart I have sought You; Oh, let me not wonder from your commandments! Your Word I have written in my heart, that I might not sin against You."

We see in this answer a strong support for what we

have already discussed in chapter 7. Multiple times, it addresses the Word of God or His commandments and the important part that these treasures play in helping us cleanse our way or stay pure. I can't help but reiterate what we've already outlined in chapter 7. But the part that stands out to me from these verses is the portion that states, "With my whole heart I have sought You."

What does it look like to pursue or search after Him with a whole heart? I don't think anyone has the final answer to this outside the entire collection of His Word. This is probably why the portion of seeking Him with one's whole heart is surrounded in these verses by descriptions of being filled with His commandments through His Word. While consuming His Word, we get a glimpse of what it might be like to wholeheartedly pursue Him. Let me add another take on this.

In our hidden world of pornography use, something happens to our heart. I believe our spiritual heart weakens because we begin to doubt that our supernatural God can either break us free *or* love us if we were to somehow get free. It's as though in the depths of our shame and guilt and the daily turmoil of hiding, we "lose heart." Because of this, we think we lose the capacity to lean into Him as we only battle from our own flesh and not through the

Spirit available to us. This is why you may feel so alone in your battle with pornography. Your heart has become disconnected from the source of life. We need the blood flow that can come only through the blood of Jesus. We have life only through Him and only through His blood.

Wholeheartedness then occurs when we acknowledge that we can do nothing in our flesh and that our heart comes alive again only through Him. His blood flowing into our hearts is always available, but too often, we try to go it alone, and we have seen where that gets us. When we connect to His heart, our heart begins to feel again, often something we have lost as we hide ourselves behind pornography. Feeling again means there is life again, and that also means there is hope again.

So as we begin to feel our heart beating again, it is all about us seeking Him, and Psalm 119 tells us to do this with all our heart. This takes me back to earlier in the chapter, where we considered our willingness scale to pursue Him. We must find clarity in our spirit that we will not experience all that we can in Him until we see that all of us is necessary to fully connect with the Lord. The answer to the question of what wholeheartedness is will be unique to every person, but I will tell you, there is always more than what you are originally willing to give. Go beyond what you think is enough, not because what Jesus did on the cross needs more of our effort but because pursuing Him will always fill us with more of Him.

You see, we are all going to be wholehearted in something, right? Some may call it committed or surrendered, but we hand ourselves over to what is most important to us. We see athletes whose schedules, diets, and routines are fully committed to their improvement and being the best at their chosen sport. You know of musicians who practice their craft and give every component of their lives to being "successful." Or what about the business owner who gives their whole self, a lot of hours and emotion to growing their business?

Whatever we give our heart to will affect our body, mind, and actions. Looking at these examples, we may think some are extreme in their commitment. That's the whole point here: *Your commitment to wholeheartedness needs to be extreme so you can enjoy the full benefits that come from the pursuit.* The human heart longs to be fully committed to something larger than itself—and no, I'm not talking about the local political initiative. I'm talking about something far more important. Wholeheartedly seeking Jesus is a real pursuit, and it is vital to living a life of freedom and purity.

Having a target of what wholeheartedness may look like gives you something to aspire to. Paul tells us, "Imitate me, just as I also imitate Christ" (1 Corinthians 11:1 NKJV). Not only is it OK to do so, it is sometimes helpful to have role models in your journey who are seeking Christ. As we have grown to know Josiah throughout the first part of this book, I think it's also helpful that we put him in this category. We should do this not only for what we have seen him do to change an entire country's culture but also because of how he was remembered. Sometimes we need to think backward from our life—how do we want to be remembered?

Josiah was remembered with these words: "Now before him there was no king like him, who turned to the Lord with all of his heart, with all of his soul, and with all of his might, according to all the Law of Moses; nor after him did any arise like him" (2 Kings 23:25 NKJV). Isn't that a life worth pursuing? That is something I would dream of being said about me. What about you? Instead of thinking forward about your life, what you want to do and accomplish, is to think backward about how you would like to be remembered, and then live forward toward your epitaph.

One vital component of being wholehearted is surrendering to the Holy Spirit. Of course, anyone reading this will have their own interpretation and history with this part of the Trinity, but as it relates to freedom and having a new way to live, I don't see any better way forward than walking with the Spirit.

Coming forth from the dungeon of pornography use is a huge transition in your life. For however long while you were imprisoned, your sinful flesh dictated every decision, and probably set new priorities in your life as well. The immense power available to you from the Holy Spirit during this time is amazing for reasons we will discuss, but first, know that the Spirit supports you by helping you to define the new freedom available to you.

Sections of Romans 8 (NKJV) impart some very powerful truths:

> There is therefore now no condemnation
> to those who are in Christ Jesus, who
> do not walk according to the flesh, but
> according to the Spirit ... For those who

live according to the flesh set their minds on the things of the flesh, but those who live according to the Spirit the things of the Spirit … But you are not in the flesh but in the Spirit, if indeed the Spirit of God dwells in you … For if you live according to the flesh you will die; but if by the Spirit you put to death the deeds of the body, you will live.

Galatians 5:16–17 (NKJV) says, "Walk in the Spirit, and you shall not fulfill the lusts of the flesh. For the flesh lusts against the Spirit, and the Spirit against the flesh; and these are contrary to one another, so that you do not do the things that you wish." It goes on to give us a list of those things that are works of the flesh (Galatians 5:19–21) and the corresponding fruits of the Spirit (Galatians 5:22–23).

So if the Holy Spirit is so important to my freedom walk and quieting my flesh, what does He do, and how do I accept His assistance? The Holy Spirit is a great mystery on purpose. He is often characterized as a wind that blows, and you don't know where He begins or ends or exactly from which direction He is blowing. John 14–16 is very profound and absolutely helpful in our quest to learn about the Holy Spirit, and I encourage you to study it thoroughly. For our time in this chapter, I will highlight three things that the Holy Spirit promises to bring you, and as someone coming forth from the slime of pornography, you will appreciate each of them as pure oxygen pumped into your depleted lungs.

First, the Holy Spirit promises to help you, and boy, do you need help. Jesus says in John 14:26 (NKJV), "The Helper, the Holy Spirit, whom the Father will send in My name, He will teach you all things, and bring to your remembrance all things that I said to you." One of the primary names of the Holy Spirit is Helper, and He will do just that for you as you ask Him.

Second, the Holy Spirit is truth—something you may have been lacking for quite a while now. Jesus says in John 16:13 (NKJV), "When He, the Spirit of truth, has come, He will guide you into all truth." The Holy Spirit has another name, Spirit of Truth, and as someone breaking out of the world where the truth became lies and the lies, truth, you could benefit from a massive dose of truth from the Spirit.

Lastly, the Holy Spirit will pray for you. Romans

8:26–27 (NKJV; emphasis mine) says, "Likewise the Spirit also helps in our weaknesses. For we do not know what we should pray for as we ought, but the Spirit Himself makes intercession for us with groanings which cannot be uttered. Now He who searches the hearts knows what the mind of the Spirit is because *He makes intercession for the saints according to the will of God.*" Not only does the Holy Spirit provide you a Helper to come alongside you and a lot of truth to help fill your depleted truth tanks, but He also cares enough about you that He has signed up to be on your own personal prayer team.

Yes, the Holy Spirit is praying for you right now, and most importantly, He is praying for you according to the will of God! Slow down for just a moment, close your eyes, and let that sink into your heart.

Let me wrap up this little section by declaring two truths vital to this time of your life. First, the life you have been living in pornography has been set up to destroy you—I mean *completely* destroy you. Fortunately, Jesus gave His life to save you. John 3:16 (NKJV) says, "For God so loved the world that He gave his only begotten Son, that whoever believes in Him should not perish but have everlasting life." Everlasting life is on the menu for you. You can choose it at any time by making Jesus Lord of your life for either the first time or as a recommitment to Him. The second truth I will conclude with is that the Holy Spirit was sent to walk out your new life with you.

Galatians 6:7–8 (NKJV) says, "Do not be deceived, God is not mocked; for whatever a man sows, that he will also reap. For he who sows to his flesh will of the flesh reap corruption, but he who sows to the Spirit will of the Spirit reap everlasting life." The everlasting life promised to you is profound, in that you not only have access to this forever, but you also have access to a better way of living *now*, with the Holy Spirit guiding your steps. Simply put, you have access to the Holy Spirit at the moment of salvation, but you also have the choice of continually being filled by the Spirit as you continually draw near to Him and pursue all that He has for you.

So finally, what does wholeheartedness look like for you? As you consider that question for yourself, let me leave you with a passage of scripture that will help you to formulate your response. I would encourage you to read these verses very slowly, and multiple times to get the full meaning of all that He is sharing with you.

Romans 6:9–14 (TPT) says,

> And we know that since the Anointed One has been raised from the dead to die no more, His resurrection life has vanquished death and its power over Him is finished. For by His sacrifice, He died to sin's power once and for all, but He now lives continuously for the Father's pleasure. So let it be the same way with you! Since you are now joined with Him, you must continually view yourselves as dead and unresponsive to sin's appeal while living daily for God's pleasure in union with Jesus, the Anointed One. Sin is a dethroned monarch; so, you must no longer give it an opportunity to rule over your life, controlling how you live and compelling you to obey its desires and cravings. So then, refuse to answer it's call to surrender your body as a tool for wickedness. Instead, passionately answer God's call to keep you yielding your body to Him as one who has now experienced

resurrection life! You live now for His pleasure, ready to be used for His noble purpose. Remember this: sin will not conquer you, for God already has! You are not governed by law but governed by the reign of the grace of God.

FREEDOM PLAN:
PURSUE WHOLEHEARTEDNESS

Contemplate: Read Psalm 119:9–11. Describe to yourself what wholeheartedness looks like and what it would take to be this way with your pursuit of Jesus. Get specific as it relates to your life, your schedule, and your unique situation. Pick one of the verses used in this chapter and take the time to write about what it means to you.

Answer: What does wholeheartedness look like to you? How would you define wholeheartedness?

What are five characteristics or traits of wholeheartedness you want to start pursuing today? Of those five, which one is of the highest importance, and how can you prioritize it in your life?

Are there any particular parts of your day, in the past, that compelled or enabled you to dabble with pornography? How can you strengthen yourself against that portion of the day or get help to fight the temptation?

What areas of your life would you consider weak in terms of your being wholehearted for Christ? How would you strengthen them?

Pray: Dear Father, my desire is to know You and learn from You. I have been a weakling regarding being Yours alone. I have given myself over to many other things and classified them as my priority. I have been soft in having clear lines of loving You fully. Please forgive me for this. Help me, Lord, to have You as my undivided pursuit, my focus, my daily desire. Lift me up to see You clearly. In Jesus's name. Amen.

Why Even Go Near the Door?

In Proverbs 5, Solomon talks to his sons to warn them against adultery. He talks about how the tempter wanders, leading any and all astray.

Solomon says in Proverbs 5:7–12 (NIV, emphasis added), "Now then, my sons, listen to me; do not turn aside from what I say, *Keep to a path far from her, do not go near the door of her house,* lest you lose your honor to others and your dignity to the one who is cruel, lest strangers feast on your wealth and your toil enrich the house of another. At the end of your life, you will groan, when your flesh and your body are spent. You will say, 'How I hated discipline! How my heart spurned correction!'"

To find true freedom from lust, we must look at our lives and find the areas that have kept us "near the door" of sexual sin. The "door" could be social media, unhealthy sexual relationships, staying up too late, or simply putting yourself in battles over your sexual purity that you have a high chance of losing. Put simply, if it can draw you into sexual sin, then it's a "door" we cannot risk being around. We don't want to be near the door, on the street, in the neighborhood, or even in the city where we can stumble into sexual sin. Take a closer look at your life. Notice the habits, tendencies, and schedules that have kept you near these doors and determine what needs to be redirected.

Don't go near the door.

CHAPTER 9

SERVE THE LORD, SERVE OTHERS

IN RESPONSE TO living a new life, free from the bondage of pornography, it is imperative that healing in many different areas takes place. As I stated in chapter 4, where I candidly discuss repentance and confession for your sins related to pornography use, there are layers of people and myriads of messes from your previous life to clean up.

Let's be very clear here: If you've never seen it stated very clearly, life in pornography is always going to be based on selfishness, lies, deceit, and hiding, among many other things. All these components leave a trail of tears and pain because of the way you have treated everyone—from the Lord to the many people who have loved you during those dark days, as well as yourself. Cleaning up everything with your Savior, spouse, children, friends, and other family members is a necessary pursuit—one that can be time-consuming yet extremely important for those relationships and your future with these lovely people.

Selfishness can be the primary magnet that draws you toward pornography. Everything about this evil world is about you—the time you spend, the need for privacy, the emotions involved, the pursuit of personal pleasure, etc. Nothing has to do with the needs or concerns of another person. The deeper you go, the more you move away from the real world where relationships require compromise, sharing, patience, and care. As a matter of fact, life with pornography can go so far in stripping away relational necessities from you that it can end up rewriting your relational hard drive with more and more selfish pursuits and expectations. The farther you go, the more you think that you *deserve* to have a secret world based solely on your evil pursuits.

The downward spiral takes you from a world you share with others to a dark place where you think only of yourself. It is in this place that you may not even recognize how selfish you have become or even believe someone if they were to point out your selfish moments throughout any given day. Nothing could be truer than Romans 8:5 (TPT), which says, "Those who are motivated by the flesh only pursue what benefits themselves. But those who live by the impulses of the Holy Spirit are motivated to pursue spiritual realities."

Not only is this occurring with you and your human relationships, but worse yet, you are doing the same thing to your relationship with the Lord. This is why this portion of your freedom plan is very important because this is the section that invites you into rewiring the life lie that it is all about you. I invite you as a part of your freedom plan to run away from selfishness. This is reinforced even more in James 3:16 (NKJV), which says, "For where envy and self-seeking exist, confusion and every evil thing are there." Is that not the case in your selfish pursuit of pornography? *Run away from selfishness.*

One way that I found to be helpful in this is by doing the opposite. I understand that this is not profound, but when you purposely pursue the opposite of selfishness, which is service, you are forced to come face-to-face with how selfish you have become. Pursuing true acts of service on your own, and informing people around you of your desire to do this, places you in a position of serving as a means of flipping the switch on selfishness. Initially, this will feel foreign to you, and possibly a bit hypocritical, because your response system is so used to receiving that giving may make you feel awkward.

One of the reasons I believe that service is so important, beyond moving away from selfishness, is that we see this as an example with Josiah. We can't seem to get away from this young king and his story, can we? You remember the story: He begins to follow the Lord at a young age, and because that was so contrary to the previous generation's way of living, he had to completely destroy and crush all the idols and images that were used for worship in those generations. Remember as well that the high priest found the Book of the Law in the temple that was being refurbished after those generations' defilement of the place for worshiping Yahweh.

When the Book of the Law was read to Josiah in 2 Chronicles 34 (NKJV), he tore his clothes in response to the words of the law that the Israelites were obviously not following. His next step was to gather all the elders of Judah and Jerusalem, along with all the priests and all the people, those "great and small" (2 Chronicles 34:30), and he read all of the Book of the Law to them. Afterward, he made a covenant before the Lord to follow Him and keep His commandments with all his heart and his soul. He then invited all the people to join him in this pursuit and he also "made all who were present in Israel *diligently serve the Lord their God*" (2 Chronicles 34:33; emphasis mine).

You see, Josiah knew something that we must learn: After generations (or in our cases with pornography, decades or years or months) of worshiping idols, there was a great need to move from selfishness to service. Serving the Lord after however long you may have found yourself in the pit of pornography is a vital next step because you are claiming anew that you will serve the Lord and not yourself any longer. Josiah and the people showed us a great example of this.

Examples of switching selfishness for service can be seen in every area of our lives, and *producing examples is important*. In Matthew 3 (AMP), John the Baptist said to the religious leaders, "Produce fruit that is consistent with repentance." As you repent and turn toward another way of living, there should be fruit that proves there has been change. Serving others are pieces of fruit that show that change has occurred.

Regarding serving, you may want to start with smaller, more mundane areas because your serving muscles are atrophied (wash the dishes, follow through on what you have said, be reliable again, fold clean clothes and put them away, take care of the yard, be available, etc.). Once you begin to get a few reps of service under your belt (and get over the fact that you're not going to be noticed and applauded for everything you do), you can move on to some bigger types of service. Bigger forms of service include consistently going out of your way to help others who can't do anything for you in return or taking back responsibilities that others in your house have taken over because of your selfishness and unreliability (cleaning the house, mowing the yard, running errands, doing something asked of you even if it is last minute, and so on). Even larger is the heart posture behind the service—going from doing something to get a positive response from others to serving simply because it is the right thing to do as part of loving others. Ask the Holy Spirit to guide you as you pursue ways in which to serve and care for those around you from a place of love.

Service is all about defying your flesh—and possibly

even the cultural or religious norms you have agreed with—and getting outside of yourself to do things that will help others. Operating from your flesh and calling it service means that you are looking for a reward when you serve—being acknowledged, applauded, or noticed. Some of you may have never seen your father operate from a place of real service, as it was not a practice of the generation he grew up in, while some of you simply may have grown up in a selfish man's house. All some of you may have seen is your father coming home from work and feeling validated to sit around and be served by others who may have had challenging days themselves. This must change, as it is hypocritical, and you are part of the generation of men who will choose to serve, especially when you're working to destroy the selfishness from your time with pornography.

Many of you are husbands, or desire to be husbands in the future. Christ's description of His love for the church in Ephesians 5 (AMP) is shared as a comparison to how we as husbands get to bless and care for our wives. Obviously, as we come out of our addiction to pornography and learn to live a new life, there is an enormous amount of healing that our wives will go through because of our sins and the painful places we have put them. Your patience and humility during this time are invaluable in your support of them as they process their own feelings.

First of all, they are in no way to be blamed for the decisions you have made. Period. Remember, it is because of you that they are having to go through this difficult time. They didn't ask for it. Take the time and invest the energy necessary to navigate this new territory together. This is often best done with a trained counselor to guide you both toward personal healing and the healing of your marriage. These are important days to go through, so prioritize this and choose humility as your default response.

Ephesians 5:25–30 (AMP) says,

> Husbands, love your wives (seek the highest good for her and surround her with a caring, unselfish love), just as Christ also loved the church and gave Himself up for her, so that He might sanctify the church, having cleansed her by the washing of water with the word (of God), so that (in turn) He might present the church to Himself in glorious splendor,

without spot or wrinkle or any such thing; but that she would be holy (set apart for God) and blameless. Even so husbands should and are morally obligated to love their own wives as (being in a sense) their own bodies. He who loves his own wife loves himself. For no one ever hated his own body, but (instead) he nourishes and protects and cherishes it, just as Christ does the church, because we are members (parts) of His body.

As I read these verses, I find it amazing that a man's life with pornography is the direct opposite of what God designed for husbands. We are to love our wives like Christ loves the church. This verse should have a powerful impact on you as you recognize who you have been as a husband and the man the Lord invites you to become. These verses are all about serving, seeking the best for your wife, cleansing her with the Word of God, protecting her, and cherishing her. All these words and phrases are the antithesis of selfishness, which, as we have already stated, is a foundational part of pornography use. We must take a step back as it relates to how we care for our spouses and rate ourselves as to how we serve them. No one is looking for perfection, but has there been progress? Are you more willing than before to lay down your life for her—not only in a figurative sense but also in the hundreds of daily ways that you can offer her a blessing by being a man of service?

Let me offer a practical example straight from Ephesians 5. It says in verse 26 that the Lord has cleansed and washed the church with his Word, and if we as husbands are to do the same with our wives, what would that look like? I would propose that we allow the Lord to show us how we can uniquely and lovingly do this with our wives. *Deep spiritual things will occur if we were to take the time and the humility necessary to read the Word of God over our spouses.* I have received the blessing of reading over my wife for decades now.

As a matter of fact, last night I asked her how many hours of our life she thinks I have read over her, and we laughed at what the answer could be because we knew it would be *a lot.* This was not always the case, though, since as a younger man, I resisted doing this out of my own shame, wounds, and insecurities. I look back wishing to have those years back, if for no other reason than to wash her with the Word of God, just like Jesus does with us.

I encourage you to make this a part of your daily interactions with your wife. How about doing this in the morning and at night? I would offer that doing this would bring about a closeness and healing that is good for both of you. Again, don't get caught up in what passages to read because the Word does its thing in the atmosphere around you and in the hearts of those we read over. Don't get caught up in how long or how "anointed" the time may be. Cleanse your spouse by washing her with the Word.

As you consider this component of your freedom plan, there will be many aspects of your life that will need to change. Moving from a life of complete selfishness to one where you desire to give and serve is a mammoth undertaking. The Lord will be with you as you are transformed. Engaging in all the pieces of the freedom plan at once will help you because each one supports the others. Make the move from selfishness to service. It will completely change how you live as it increases the relational aspect of who the Lord has made you as well as aid you in destroying the man you used to be who was lost in selfishness.

FREEDOM PLAN:
SERVE THE LORD AND OTHERS

Contemplate: Take a time inventory during this week of your life. Journal moments where selfishness ruled over your day, either by your actions or simply by your thoughts. Maybe you got angry when something didn't go your way or frustrated that you had to pick up the slack of someone else at work or at home. List these selfish moments and write a corresponding servant response to consider for the future.

Answer: How would you define service or serving? Go beyond a dictionary definition. How would you explain it to someone? What examples would you use to define it?

What are three to five specific areas at home, at work, and at your church where you can commit to acts of service this next week? Track these to see if you followed through on your commitment.

Who is someone that you would classify as a servant? What are the three characteristics that stand out to you about this person that reinforce their servant lifestyle? How could these characteristics be transferable to you?

Pray: Jesus, please come to me now. I have been so selfish and thought everything revolved around me. The more I look at myself, the more I notice that I have become a selfish person, and my pornography use has only been gasoline thrown on the fire of my self-absorption. Lord, please turn my gaze away from myself and allow me to see You clearly. Help me to see service as a joy and a blessing and that giving is more fulfilling than pursuing my own desires.

Prayer Workouts

I once heard a pastor say that it's interesting that we don't think of our time as something that we should tithe to the Lord. We sometimes give Him everything else in our lives, and yet give Him a mere ten to twenty minutes to encounter us in the morning as we rush out the door. If we were to give God 10 percent of our time each day, wouldn't it be two hours and twenty-four minutes? Time is a huge commodity, and we get to determine how we use it.

Engaging in sexual sin, especially through porn and masturbation, is the single most selfish act that a human can do, and it takes up time too. In the midst of that selfishness, I have found a direct correlation between selflessly praying for others and continuously having victory in my personal sexual life. So, in pursuit of more victories, I began to wonder how I could find time to pray for others because I knew it also helped me in return.

Like most of us, I have struggled to stay focused in my time with the Lord and to pray for others too. One of the places where I have a lot of time available in the day is when I work out. One day I was trying to squeeze in my Bible time before going to the gym when I had a thought: *Why don't I structure this time how I structure a workout?* This has been a huge help for me to keep my time focused and efficient. Feel free to design your prayer workout however you would like, but here is an example:

—Ten minutes in the Word
—Five minutes praying for your family

—Five minutes praying for your friends

—Five minutes praying for your church/community

—Five minutes just waiting quietly on the Lord

This is a great way to get outside yourself and focus on others and their needs, knowing that in return, you will receive victory over lust during that time too.

Stay strong!

CHAPTER 10

DEVELOP A NEW LIFE
AND DAILY SCHEDULE

ONE INTEGRAL PART of moving forward after a life in pornography is to make changes to certain aspects of your day to the point where you are almost living a brand-new life. In a world where your pornography pursuits defined what you thought about yourself, your relationships, and your schedule, it is vital that you establish a hard reset and live from a different place. You should not be surprised that living a life with pornography would not impact every aspect of your life.

Galatians 6:7–9 (NKJV) says, "Do not be deceived, God is not mocked; for whatever a man sows, that he will also reap. For he who sows to his flesh will of the flesh reap corruption, but he who sows to the Spirit will of the Spirit reap everlasting life. And let us not grow weary while doing good, for in due season we shall reap if we do not lose heart." For instance, if I were to plant a cucumber seed in our garden, would I be surprised if it produced bananas? Of course, I would be. It's the same thing with how we live our lives: How we spend our time will determine the fruit of our lives.

As you well know, living a life full of pornography use is a life of chaos. As you sought to have a place where you thought you were in total control, you found out that you were deep into the extreme opposite. What we thought we could control had taken control over us. It is so important that as we begin to take the steps toward a new life, we must prioritize our destination more than the wind of the moment. Those winds of your pornography use that we initially labeled as exciting increased without our noticing, and all of a sudden, you found yourself in a hurricane. Focus on your destination, which is Christ, and keep Him as your focal point, and you will notice quickly if you are being blown off course in any way.

As you know, life with pornography is full of lies, deceit, and hiding. Part of establishing a new life in

Christ is to repent and confess of your sins (see chapter 4) and to make changes not only in how you think but also in how you live. Colossians 3 (NKJV) offers guidance on this topic.

Colossians 3:2–3 says, "Set your mind on things above, not on things on the earth. For you died, and your life is hidden with Christ in God."

Verse 5 says, "Therefore put to death your members which are on the earth: fornication, uncleanness, passion, evil desire, and covetousness, which is idolatry."

Verses 9–10 says, "Do not lie to one another, since you have put off the old man with his deeds, and have put on the new man who is renewed in knowledge according to the image of Him who created him."

As we choose Christ and His way of living, we kill off the works of our flesh. Part of this occurs when we give up our previous way of living, but more importantly, we change our focus and our destination. When we set our minds on things above and not on the earth, we are forced to reconsider every single decision that we make every day. Paul says very clearly that we "put to death" those things in us that are earthly focused and earthly bound. Why? So we can set our minds on the things above. As it says in Matthew 6:24 (NKJV), "No one can serve two masters; for either he will hate the one and love the other, or else he will be loyal to the one and despise the other."

Either we choose to live in the flesh—and for many of us, this means pornography and the sexual cesspool it creates—or we kill off the flesh and choose Him totally and completely. That means all the aspects surrounding pornography must be destroyed as well. All the lying and hiding that has become our way of coping have to end, along with our actual pornography use. This leads us to the picture we find in verses 9–10.

In these vivid verses, we see the holy transformation that takes place as an old man dies and a new man emerges. This is the picture of a new life: It's not one or the other occurring—it is both occurring at the same time that allows a full transformation to activate.

Jerod was a great example of this. After initially getting tagged by his employer for misusing the company's internet access for pornography searches and almost getting fired, he woke up to where this struggle had gotten him. His aggressive response to the change in his way of living included many of the freedom plan components, but especially this one. All at once, he pursued a thorough purging of who he had become, scrubbing the terrible foundation of what he was doing while taking this moment to return to the church he had previously stopped attending. He was effectively dealing with evil while also filling his time with better influences, which allowed him to attack his situation from both extremes. The outcome was a better person—and for his company, a better employee.

Another verse that amplifies this is found in 2 Corinthians 5:17 (NKJV), which states, "Therefore, if anyone is in Christ, he is a new creation; old things have passed away; behold, all things have become new." I love the statue *Born Again* by Dean Kermit Allison, which is a visual representation of what is really occurring in our spirit as we die to the flesh and become alive in Christ. I would encourage you to check this out.

When I mentioned the importance of developing a new life as part of your freedom plan, I am talking about you becoming someone you may not even recognize. I'm talking about those around you seeing a new person who acts differently, and maybe even looks different. I'm talking about a dead man rising up and choosing a better way to live, a better way to love those around him, and a better way to love the Lord. I find it interesting that in 1 Samuel 10 (NKJV), when Saul had been anointed as the first king of Israel, the description was that "the Spirit of the Lord came upon him" and "he turned into another man." In other words, he took on a different countenance, which brought about a different outcome. This example is available to us as we also come to the Lord and are turned into a new man.

One aspect of a person's exit from a life consumed by pornography is the emotional reignition that will eventually occur. While in the prison of pornography, we most assuredly lose touch with our emotions because we are totally and completely consumed with ourselves and with hiding. We stop caring for ourselves and others, as we are only looking for the next moment that we can get lost in our hiding place with pornography. Coming to life on the other side is full of breakthroughs, and among the greatest of them is a rekindling of the embers of care or concern for self and others. The selfishness involved in pornography addiction puts a wet blanket over the passionate fire of love and relationships, so having a new life on the other side allows that holy fire to be reignited and eventually roar again. This fire in our bones allows us to see the

Lord for who He is, our sin for what it is, and those who love us for who they are.

The emotional reignition will be unique for everyone, but it will almost always include deep feelings of remorse and loss, a desire to correct all the areas in which you have failed, and tears, oh so many tears. As you enter a new life, you will be shocked at what can trigger your emotions. Sometimes it may be the smallest thing that brings about the sobbing. These are signs that your emotional dam is breaking and that you are coming to life again. This reigniting of your emotions will be something that you will be so blessed to reacquaint yourself with, and you will begin to see progress because you are feeling again.

As you develop a new life centered around your daily schedule, there will be a number of more practical decisions to consider. It is in the activation of a new life that your priorities change, and this trickles all the way down to how you choose to fill the hours of your day. In the past, where your pornography pursuits were the columns that your schedule was balancing upon (very wobbly, I'm sure), I recommend that your day be built upon the columns of Spirit, Soul, and Body. Of course, I do not see these as equally necessary for life as the spiritual category is of the highest priority now and always.

I would recommend that you plot your daily schedule on how your spirit is fed, nourished, and supported. Think about how you can nurture your spiritual development as you consider your daily schedule. For many, it is vital to start your day with the study of the Word and prayer, and I think that should be a foundational consideration. Starting your day in Him increases your chances of being in Him throughout the day. But maybe you need to go farther. Maybe every hour you need five minutes to pray and read a few verses from the Bible. Possibly, if you are one who is car-bound throughout the day, choose podcasts that nourish your spirit, or skip sports talk radio and fill your time with the spoken Word or an audible book from a Christian author.

I wholeheartedly recommend that you find ways to do these types of things with your spouse and family, or with your friends if you're not married. All of this is to reignite the fire in your spirit, which died off during your days in pornography. Use your schedule as a reminder to do beneficial things that help to keep you alive.

Your daily schedule considerations related to soul and body should be established with the same thought to holy order in your life. Your soul (mind, will, emotions, intellect, and memory) will come to life with beneficial activities such as journaling your breakthroughs with the Lord, memorizing scripture, singing songs that put your focus on the Lord, as well as having thoughtful conversations with believers who will stretch you and cause you to study the Word for answers. In addition, prioritizing things that help your body grow and heal throughout your daily schedule is important too. The things you need to consider for your body include the amount and schedule of rest/sleep, physical exercise, quality of nutritional plans, and consistency of stress-reducing activities. All these are important. It's also amazing how your spirit, soul, and body activities cross-benefit each other as you develop a new schedule for a new you.

The reason that I emphasize building your daily schedule with these columns of spirit, soul, and body is that you are coming out of a life where you had no order except what pornography compelled you to do. This shift in your daily schedule from anything goes to highly regimented is initially focused on restoring order and prioritizing the good things you need in your life over the desires of your flesh. As you operate in a more focused daily pursuit, you will begin to notice a stability and refocusing that will affect you in a very positive way. This initial highly structured pursuit focusing on spirit, soul, and body is not established to be worshiped but as a tool that helps you reset your life and positions you to move forward in healing and strength.

One of the main reasons I am placing so much emphasis on our daily schedule is that we must set new battle lines and our schedule is the primary place where this occurs. In the past, when pornography ruled you, your days and nights were dictated by the whims of the evil pull of pornography, and you gradually gave up ground in your defense, to the point where you eventually gave in completely. Your defense became so weak and pathetic that it was questionable whether you were fighting back at all. This is the reason why you need to set new battle lines, and this is determined by how we apportion the minutes and hours of each day.

Breaking forth from the control of pornography begins by giving it no time in your schedule. I know that seems too simple, but remember that you were once a person who took care of yourself, shared yourself with others, and pursued a vibrant relationship with Jesus and then you gave a moment to pornography. Initially, it was only a quick click or a quick glance that took up less than a minute of your day. As you gradually called your defense off the field, you allowed the pornography demon to run all over you; but it began with you giving it time. We are now going to learn how to take back that time in your schedule, and this is an example of setting new battle lines.

Think back to the days of battle as you see in movies like *Braveheart*, where it is basically hand-to-hand combat. In these battles one side never set their battle line right next to their enemy, they would set their line far enough back to notice any attack as it was developing. Your battle lines can be as basic as how you spend every *moment* of your day, but it can also include where you set your *boundaries* regarding what you know are triggers to your weakness to pornography, as well as who is *supporting* your progress. Basically, what I am encouraging you to do in these areas is not only go back to where you were before you opened the door to pornography, but also to build an even better battle line. I'm calling you to find out what should be the best place in which to set your battle lines.

With regard to time, establishing a new, highly defined schedule with body, soul, and spirit as your focus reorients your heart so you do not give a second of your day to dabbling with pornography. In reference to other boundaries, notice and define your triggers: They may include loneliness, isolation, fatigue, bingeing on TV, computer, phone, frustration, sadness, loss, etc., and build strong battle lines for each of these before they become an issue. Lastly, as it relates to support, go to your newly defined battle lines with other warriors who not only fight with you but also expect you to fight for them. It is a special type of strength that allows others to know everything about your life and schedule, where you are, who you're with, what you are streaming, or what sites, apps, or social media platforms you're spending time on. New battle lines in these areas are examples of you moving into an offensive posture of protection while also shoring up your defensive battle lines.

One important point as it relates to all these is the importance of surrounding yourself with others during your journey away from pornography. What I mean by this is that in the months, years, or decades you have spent consuming pornography, you have become adept at being alone. This is partly because of all the hiding that naturally occurs in relation to pornography, but even more so, you have probably taken it farther by isolating yourself and pushing others away so that no one will find you out.

Maybe you just stopped accepting invitations to be with others, stayed extra hours at work instead of going home to your family, or added extra unnecessary travel to your work simply to just be alone, to be hidden. This takes you to a place where you begin to think of yourself as an introvert, when you really just may have been a hider. Part of coming out of your pornography prison is to be around people, learning to engage in conversation, showing care for others in need of help, asking others to join you for a meal, and accepting those invitations from others that you always rejected before. A vital part of your new schedule should include other people—in the past when you looked to find ways to be alone now look for ways to join with others and live a full life.

Even further is the relational need to have accountability with those who you trust to help you in settling into a new life. As mentioned before the isolation that occurs during your pornography hibernation is your setting up things so that no one knows what you are doing and, in reality, no one knows who you are anymore. This hiding must be broken with exposure. Initially, this may occur with you finding one person you trust to expose your daily schedule to and offer full access to your life. This is part of your new daily approach to living and that is having people in your life who are real people who address the fantasy world of pornography for what it is, people you can trust to help you day by day to live a new way.

In my opinion, the person you choose to be accountable to should be another guy who you know will stretch you. Someone who will call you higher. Someone who will not allow lame excuses. Someone who will call out lies for what they are. Someone who will be content only with your full healing and success in this area of your life. You need a close comrade who will be available to you every day and at all hours. I know this may seem difficult, especially as you have spent so much of your energy moving away from others, but having a person close to you to be fully accountable to is part of breaking out of hiding, and deep down, you know you need this.

Finally, as we look at our daily schedule and develop

a new life, one of the questions I am often asked by those with a few victories with pornography goes something like this: "I have spent a good deal of time away from pornography using pieces of the freedom plan and now I think I'm ready to drop some of the safeguards I put in place when things were really bad for me—when can I drop some of my boundaries?" As often as I am asked this question, I still cannot believe the question is coming out of the person's mouth.

Let me cut to the chase on this one. I have a much longer answer, but my short one is there is nothing worth risking going back to the pit of hell we call pornography, where I would give up the ground that I have worked hard to attain just to have a few things back that I used to have. Don't forget where you used to be! My answer to this question for myself is that many of the safeguards that I have ever put in place are still in place in my life, if not stronger than they were before, and I would encourage that for you as well.

Let me give you an example: Athletes can be the worst in the world at protecting themselves from further injury. You know the stories of athletes who get injured, and because of their desire to get back in the action, they tell the doctor, "I'm OK," and they are ready to go back into the game. Athletes always need more time to heal than their minds will allow them to think. This is why many athletes return from injury too soon and eventually get injured more severely. Complete healing for the athlete and their injury or you in your healing from being consumed by pornography will always take longer than you are willing to think. Dropping too many safeguards in your battle with pornography too early is premature and leaves you with way too little to gain and way too much to lose. When safeguards are put in place and are found to be effective, you should really ask the question as to whether the safeguard should be removed *at all*, or if they should become your new normal and operate your battle line from this new position of victory.

Lastly, as we wrap up this chapter on developing a new life and a new schedule, let me leave you with a key verse in the Bible to use as you establish a new way to live. One of the best-known chapters in the Bible, 1 Corinthians 13, focuses on love. This chapter is powerful and full of reminders for us in how to love others, and I recommend you take a closer look. One key verse in chapter 13 that stands out to me as it relates to developing a new life is verse 11 (NKJV): "When I was a child, I spoke as a child, I understood as a child, I thought as a child; but when I became a man, I put away childish things." In many ways, as we step out of pornography use, we are like children who want to grow up but don't know how to yet.

In this verse, we see the importance of putting away childish things as we grow up to be men, and it gives us examples in three areas. The first area is how we *speak*. As we outgrow our pursuit of pornography, we will need to grow up in this area because our speech has been heavily influenced by blaming, lies, curses and cursing, excuses, and deception. We have spoken as one who didn't know any better when in reality we did, and we chose not to speak from a place of maturity. A second example this verse gives us of changes made as we grow up is in how we *understand* situations. In our days and nights with pornography, we made certain decisions and judgments, and more often than not, we did not take responsibility for these immature and irresponsible thoughts. We understood our situation as "not being that bad" or "not as bad as others" and justified our pursuits with the understanding of an infant.

Lastly, we must grow up in terms of how we *think*. In

the sewer of pornography, we completely disregarded reflection, contemplation, and consideration of the outcomes of our actions. We did not think, period. So just as He does regarding our speech and our understanding, the Lord invites us to put away immaturity as it relates to our thoughts. Change and growth in these three areas will lead us into a new life and a desire for a new daily schedule.

Let's cut to the chase: When coming out of the control of pornography, we need almost everything to be new. How we have chosen to operate, and the crumbling of our boundaries have virtually destroyed us. Starting anew means destroying what has bound you and considering what can be new in every area of your life. This is a perfect time for a wholesale inventory of who you are, how you got there, and where you want to end up. Lay everything out on the table. Check everything as to whether it has been beneficial to you. Invite the voices of those who love you to speak in this 360-degree review. Become new, whole, and pure again.

FREEDOM PLAN: DEVELOP A NEW LIFE AND DAILY SCHEDULE

Contemplate: As you leave behind a life in pornography, which was based on lies, and begin to pursue a new life—or better yet, the life He established you to live—consider everything that goes into your day. Think about how you determine what is to be included in your day. Consider how you prioritize certain things over other things. Reflect on who else gets to speak about what your daily schedule looks like.

Answer: In your pursuit of freedom from pornography, what would a "perfect day" look like? Go hour by hour on a typical day and describe what that day would look like free from pornography and sexual diversions. If you followed the schedule of that "perfect day," how would you feel about yourself at the end of the day?

What do you want the new you to be like? What areas must you change and grow in to become the person you desire to be? How does the order of your day coincide with this?

Who are the people that you will invite into the scheduling of your day so that any blind spots are noticed and addressed or just to provide another perspective on how you use your time?

Pray: Holy Father, thank you for caring for me even when I have not cared for myself. Thank you for being a God of order and structure and offering those to me as well. The ways in which I have lived my life up to this point have not been good, and in many ways, they have been damaging. Please come into my life, every minute of my life, and show me how to live and how to make decisions. Your ways are perfect, and I need You.

Why Fight Unnecessary Battles?

Why make the battle harder than it already is? An alcoholic who is in recovery is obviously not going to spend time at a bar, so why is it that those of us in recovery from sexual sin continue to hang around areas filled with temptation? These areas disguised as social media, YouTube, news sites, or even the music that we listen to aren't necessarily threatening on the outside; but for me, and possibly you, they are potential snares. An unnecessary battle is one where you willingly put yourself in danger and where there is simply nothing to gain and everything to lose. Examples in our purity lives include a movie or a TV show that has any degree of sexual trash in it, or social media accounts of a similar nature.

The great military strategist, Sun Tzu once said, "The wise warrior avoids the battle."

Think of the past few times that you have slipped up and try to pinpoint the exact moment that made you start going in that direction. Odds are, you encountered something sexual, probably without going out of your way to intentionally see something sexual. This is life. But we do have more control over this than we think! If you are serious about redirecting your life, you must be willing to make huge changes in it. Start by cutting out the avenues that have led you into this sexual sin. Go one week with no socials, or a week with no YouTube—whatever it is for you, begin with a short time away from it, and I bet, in the near future, you can look back and see how that decision affected your walk in purity in a positive way.

Rees

CHAPTER 11

SHARE YOUR STORY

AS ONE STEPS out of the self-destructive life of pornography use, there is typically a humility that accompanies the exit. Either because of the public nature to which you were exposed or the overwhelming recognition of who you have become, I hope that you would embrace a certain degree of humbleness. Humility is a good place for us to operate, but it will either be chosen by us or pressed upon us. You will get through the embarrassment that comes with either forced or chosen exposure, but I would encourage you to make the decision to move forward apart from pornography instead of being forced which can be more public and painful. When you choose humility, you are choosing life, not only for yourself but also for those you love.

I am constantly reminded of the great gift that Jesus gave me by dying on the cross to pay for my sins. I know that He did this for all of mankind, but it is sometimes good for us to personalize this, especially when we are stepping into a new life apart from pornography. It says in 1 Corinthians 6:20 (NKJV), "For you were bought at a price; therefore, glorify God in your body and in your spirit, which are God's." This verse is such a great reminder of who I belong to. Life with pornography is full of selfishness, but I was saved so that my body and my spirit can glorify Him. This recognition of Christ dying on the cross for you alone personalizes His sacrifice and increases the potential for you to choose humility. This can grow in you whether you chose to escape the clutches of pornography or whether you were caught and initially acted without humility. What Christ has done for us is available to people in both scenarios.

Let me be clear here before moving forward. There is a difference between choosing to step out of pornography on your own and those who are exposed and feel that their only choice is to pull away from pornography out of duty. The second group must determine why they are pulling away—is it to appease those who exposed them, or is it a sincere moving away from pornography? Those who choose to repent of their sin of pornography use have an initial humility that sets them on the path to freedom that the other person can't prove yet. For those who were "forced" out, they must make the choice as to whether this time it is real for them. This component is so important in stepping away from pornography as it is only through humility, and implementing all aspects of your freedom plan, that you will succeed.

All of this leads to the topic of this chapter which focuses on sharing your story. There is a lot that goes into sharing what you have been through as an overcomer of pornography. Revelation 12:11 (AMP) says, "They overcame and conquered him because of the blood of the Lamb and because of the word of their testimony." Stepping out of pornography and overcoming the evil one occurs by the blood of Jesus and the use of our testimonies. Our experiences of glorifying God through our redemption stories are huge in the heavenly realm. Sharing what you have gone through with others is good not only for them but also for you, as well. There are many factors to consider as you move toward sharing your story.

One of the challenges I've noticed related to our testimony is that those who are less than a minute out of pornography are either testifying about their "freedom" to either appease someone who caught them or prematurely testifying out of the excitement that comes when in the vicinity of freedom. Trust me, those who are caught in pornography are willing to do just about anything, including testify, to get those who caught them back in their good graces. Also, those who are excited about the possibility of freedom but who have not won many battles yet and quickly testify can get their knees cut out from under them when they give in to the temptation to return to pornography use. Either way, there is good reason to be measured when using this aspect of your testimony too soon after a small taste of freedom from pornography.

Let me try to explain that last sentence. First of all, there should be excitement about telling your story about moving away from pornography. There is reason to rejoice. There is also a need to let the cement dry a bit before stepping on it with confidence. There are ongoing stages of freedom that you will go through toward full freedom, and I would encourage you to win a few battles where you can genuinely say no to pornography before making any public appearances about your initial decision. Please hear my heart here, be excited about your freedom, but be free for a while before you go public. This is specifically important if you engage in various social media platforms where announcements are either applauded or attacked by unknown people.

Years ago, about a month after I bashed up my computer, the Lord told me that *the power is in the secret* for most men. What I gathered from this is that when men delve into pornography, they are held captive in its devices simply because of how powerful the secret is that holds them bound. Ecclesiastes 12:13–14 (NKJV) says, "Let us hear the conclusion of the whole matter: Fear God and keep His commandments, for this is man's all. For God will bring every work into judgment, Including every secret thing, Whether good or evil." The controlling aspect of any hidden sin is the secret itself.

The power that holds people in bondage is the thought that they are in this alone and it's too embarrassing, revealing, or vulnerable to let anyone know about this private world. The truth to that lie is that it is life-changing to invite other men into your secret world because they bring with them the key to unlocking the secret that holds you in silent bondage. This, I believe, is the initial first step that men should go through in terms of sharing their stories. Instead of a public announcement or social media posts about what you are currently working through, why not include one or two others you trust to help break the power of the secret? For every man who has taken this initial approach of sharing with a few others, I have never heard of them not being met with respect, support, and compassion, if not confessions from those you shared with. The power is in the secret. Reveal the secret and break its hold on you.

Breaking down the lies of the secret world allows us to see pornography for what it is, your redemption by Jesus for what it is, and the need for camaraderie with other men. Sharing our stories begins with the vulnerability of sharing it with one person. Don't get caught up in a big reveal or giving your testimony to the thousands. Be caught up in daily victories told to a small group of guys and add your victories on top of more victories to build your faith. Trust me, if you are faithful in keeping clean for days, weeks, months, and years, your story will take on a public nature because men with sustained victories are true examples in today's world. Start small in building your story, journal about what you have experienced and learned, and appropriately share your story, as it is life-giving to those who are still in bondage.

FREEDOM PLAN:
SHARE YOUR STORY

Contemplate: As you begin to engage a group of others who are supporting your freedom, consider how important this is to your success. Take the time to really engage with these guys and hear their stories, not just you telling yours. Become comfortable over time with this group explaining your highs and lows, victories and defeats, and praying with each other. As you grow in your purity and in your comfort in sharing your story, feel free to expand your level of vulnerability with others, to the point where you can give your full testimony of overcoming pornography use.

Answer: Who are the two to four other men that you trust to invite into your secret? What is holding you back from contacting them today? That is not a hypothetical question, but a very real one! If you're not willing to do this right now, then why not?

What is it that holds you back from sharing your story with other men? Are you afraid of their response? Are you struggling with trusting others?

How would you describe "the power is in the secret"? How has this played out in your life?

Pray: Merciful Father, who has cared for me and loves me, thank You for being so near. Thank You for loving me in my worst days and when I ran so far from You. Your loving kindness to me is so precious and undeserved, and I thank You for giving it to me so generously. I ask You, Holy Spirit, to counsel my heart and give me insight into the sharing of the victories You have given to me. Jesus, please let my testimony be full of Your grace, and may it help others to find freedom in You too. I love You!

Too Strong?

We're never going to be "too strong." The sooner we realize this, the sooner we will understand that we are completely helpless in this battle without the Lord's mercy and His strength. As soon as we begin to think, *Temptation doesn't really affect me anymore*—that is the exact moment when we need to lock in, get in the Word to get strong again. The moment that we get to a point where we feel like we are "safe" or "strong enough" to watch that movie or show that has sexual garbage in it is the exact moment that the enemy is moving, hunting you, trying to separate you from your plan for purity and your connection to the Lord.

The enemy wants you to get lazy. The enemy is willing to wait patiently for you to let your guard down and relax. He wants you to abandon the plans and the structure that you have set up to have freedom. The enemy wants to take your life. Remember, though, that the Lord has more in store for you. Remember that He has hope and a future in mind for you. Lock into your plan and stay humble before the Lord, because only He can release your foot from these traps (Psalm 25:15 NLT).

CONCLUSION

As I write this, there is yet another US Presidential Election on the horizon. It seems these elections come at us sooner and sooner all the time. One of the consistent messages from whichever candidate is that we live in a free country. Freedom, politically speaking, is a concept not readily appreciated by those of us who have always been free. We as free people can easily take for granted what it means because we have always had such a somewhat easy freedom. I don't think we really understand the difficulties and struggles of those who live in a place where you cannot do as you want when you want.

The only comparison some of us may ever have are the feelings when we have been completely taken over by something that overwhelms us, and we can't revert to that easy freedom. Of course, from this book, we have spoken candidly about the bondage and imprisonment we feel when we're stuck in the pit of pornography. For all who have been there, the thought of true freedom can seem impossible or out of reach because of what you have seen, done, or considered. My prayer is that through the freedom plan discussed within these pages, you have developed some traction to move forward, and you have enjoyed progress toward complete freedom. That is our desire in writing this book—that you walk in freedom, that you become the man that God intended and desires you to be, and that you help others to do the same.

I love the lyrics to UPPERROOM's song "Washed," as it seems to track so clearly with all that we've shared in this book.

The first verse goes like this:

> *When I was lost, the wayward one so far away*
> *I was Your thought, there on the cross that day*
> *I saw the feast, but I chose the dirt to lay my head*
> *I was a captive to what the accuser said*
>
> *Then You stepped into my grave*
> *Laughing at the guilt and shame*
> *And all my fear was stripped away*
> *Now I stand and sing*

I am washed by the blood of the Lamb
I am washed by the blood of the Lamb
By Your scars my sin erased I'm innocent

UPPERROOM and Brett
Bell, "Washed" *To The
One (Live)*, 2019, Apple
Music

You know we all have been lost at one time or another, and we are all so blessed that Jesus died on the cross so that we can be found and live a new life. We are all washed by the blood of the Lamb when we give ourselves over to Him and give up our life's control to His ways. This song needs to be on your playlist!

As I have been reviewing the contents of this book, I am even more convinced of its potential in a small group setting, where men can come together to grow in their faith and their purity. We live in a broken world that needs whole men to grow up and foster positive relationships with their spouses, children, and other significant people in their lives. Consider how you can share the contents of this book with your realm of influence. As you take a step forward to find freedom for yourself through this book, consider how you may be the one who can offer a lift to others who need their own freedom. We must help each other. We need Jesus.

APPENDIX

FREEDOM PLAN

- Repent/confess.
- Destroy the idols.
- Consume the Word.
- Pursue wholeheartedness.
- Serve the Lord and others.
- Develop a new life and daily schedule.
- Share your story.

FREEDOM PLAN:
REPENT/CONFESS

Contemplate: Set aside a period of time where you can process your life and experiences with pornography. Using pieces of paper or your phone, make a list of specific things you would like to turn away from as it relates to your pornography use. Be candidly clear and detailed about the things that you have found that have brought you the most pain and sorrow. Consider the things that you have tried so hard to hide, even from your own realization, and put those things on your list, as there is always something that needs to be brought to the light when you have invested so much in hiding it.

Answer: Have you repented or changed your mind about pornography? If so, what changes have you noticed in your thoughts? If not, what do you think is the wall that is holding you back?

Have you confessed to a trusted person what is really going on with your pornography use? If so, what was their response? If not, what is holding you back from doing this?

Pray: Lord, I need your help, again. I know that what I have read here is truth, and I need You to give me the courage to walk forward in this. Help me to see pornography the way You see it. Open my eyes to Your truth and help me to have Your heart. Beyond Your support, I ask, Lord, that you bring others around me to help. This is my time for freedom. Help me, Lord, in each next step. I love you, Jesus.

FREEDOM PLAN:
DESTROY THE IDOLS

Contemplate: Take ten to fifteen minutes to quietly consider how pornography is an idol for you. Look into your soul and determine how you see it, miss it, handle it, and, possibly, how you protect it. How would you define pornography's role in your life, and how does that response factor into whether or not it is an idol for you? Take the time to evaluate your schedule and your level of desire for pornography and give it a definite title. Is it an idol?

Answer: We all have certain friends that we go to first when we are in need. If pornography were to be classified as a "friend" of yours, how quickly do you go to it when you are stressed or in a "situation"?

What are the idols you would like to destroy? Be very specific. Pornography is a category. Be specific about what your idols are.

What are the corresponding supports that have kept these idols alive and active? What supports, if taken away, would cause your idols to fall?

What have been your excuses for not destroying either the idols or their supports?

Be real: How much time in a week have you given over to pornography in all its various forms?

What does destruction look like for the idols/supports you have listed?

Who else knows about your idols? Who do you trust to share this with? Go over your answers to these questions with that person and ask them to help you.

Pray: Father, my worship has not been dedicated to You. I have given myself over to another, and it is destroying my life. Please be near to me now and help me to see things the way You see them. Help me to see pornography and my setting it on a hidden precipice for what it is. I am in great need, Lord. I open my heart to You now and ask You to take over.

FREEDOM PLAN:
CONSUME THE WORD

Appetizer scriptures: Choose three to five of the scriptures below and do the following:

1. Commit them to memory.
2. Write them out by hand ten times a day.
3. Read them into your voice memos on your phone and play them four to five times a day.
4. Journal a paragraph using a different verse each day as a jumping-off spot.
5. Text a verse to someone else to encourage them.

Psalm 16:1, 16:11 (NKJV)

> Preserve me, O God, for in You I put my
> trust. … You will show me the path of life;
> In Your presence is fullness of joy; At Your
> right hand are pleasures forevermore.

Psalm 18:1–3 (NKJV)

> I will love You, O Lord, my strength. The Lord is my rock and my fortress and my deliverer; My God, my strength, in whom I will trust; My shield and the horn of my salvation, my stronghold. I will call upon the Lord, who is worthy to be praised; So shall I be saved from my enemies.

Psalm 27:1 (NKJV)

> The Lord is my light and my salvation; Whom shall I fear? The Lord is the strength of my life; Of whom shall I be afraid?

Psalm 101:3–4 (NKJV)

> I will set nothing wicked before my eyes; I hate the work of those who fall away; It shall not cling to me. A perverse heart shall depart from me;
> I will not know wickedness.

Psalm 119:9–11 (NKJV)

> How can a young man cleanse his way?
> By taking heed according to Your word.
> With my whole heart I have sought You;
> Oh, let me not wander from Your commandments!
> Your word I have hidden in my heart,
> That I might not sin against You.

Proverbs 10:9 (NKJV)

> He who walks with integrity walks securely, But he who perverts his ways will become known.

Proverbs 11:3 (NIV)

> The integrity of the upright guides them, but the unfaithful are destroyed by their duplicity.

Mark 12:28–31 (NKJV)

> Then one of the scribes came, and having heard them reasoning together, perceiving

that He had answered them well, asked Him, "Which is the first commandment of all?"

Jesus answered him, "The first of all the commandments is: 'Hear, O Israel, the Lord our God, the Lord is one. And you shall love the Lord your God with all your heart, with all your soul, with all your mind, and with all your strength.' This is the first commandment. And the second, like it, is this: 'You shall love your neighbor as yourself.' There is no other commandment greater than these."

John 8:31–32 (NKJV)

Then Jesus said to those Jews who believed Him, "If you abide in My word, you are My disciples indeed. And you shall know the truth, and the truth shall make you free."

John 8:36 (NKJV)

Therefore if the Son makes you free, you shall be free indeed.

John 10:10 (NKJV)

> The thief does not come except to steal, and to kill, and to destroy. I have come that they may have life, and that they may have it more abundantly.

Romans 8:5–6 (NKJV)

> For those who live according to the flesh set their minds on the things of the flesh, but those who live according to the Spirit, the things of the Spirit. For to be carnally minded is death, but to be spiritually minded is life and peace.

Romans 12:1–2 (NKJV)

> I beseech you therefore, brethren, by the mercies of God, that you present your bodies a living sacrifice, holy, acceptable to God, which is your reasonable service. And do not be conformed to this world, but be transformed by the renewing of your mind, that you may prove what is

that good and acceptable and perfect will
of God.

Romans 12:9 (NKJV)

Let love be without hypocrisy. Abhor
what is evil. Cling to what is good.

Romans 15:13 (NKJV)

Now may the God of hope fill you with
all joy and peace in believing, that you
may abound in hope by the power of the
Holy Spirit.

1 Corinthians 6:13 (NKJV)

Now the body is not for sexual immorality
but for the Lord, and the Lord for the body.

1 Corinthians 6:20 (NKJV)

For you were bought at a price; therefore
glorify God in your body and in your
spirit, which are God's.

1 Corinthians 10:21 (NKJV)

> You cannot drink the cup of the Lord and the cup of demons; you cannot partake of the Lord's table and of the table of demons.

1 Corinthians 13:11 (NKJV)

> When I was a child, I spoke as a child, I understood as a child, I thought as a child; but when I became a man, I put away childish things.

2 Corinthians 5:17 (NKJV)

> Therefore, if anyone is in Christ, he is a new creation; old things have passed away; behold, all things have become new.

2 Corinthians 7:10 (NKJV)

> For godly sorrow produces repentance leading to salvation, not to be regretted; but the sorrow of the world produces death.

Galatians 5:16–17 (NKJV)

I say then: Walk in the Spirit, and you shall not fulfill the lust of the flesh. For the flesh lusts against the Spirit, and the Spirit against the flesh; and these are contrary to one another, so that you do not do the things that you wish.

Galatians 6:7–9 (NKJV)

Do not be deceived, God is not mocked; for whatever a man sows, that he will also reap. For he who sows to his flesh will of the flesh reap corruption, but he who sows to the Spirit will of the Spirit reap everlasting life. And let us not grow weary while doing good, for in due season we shall reap if we do not lose heart.

Ephesians 2:1–10 (NKJV)

And you He made alive, who were dead in trespasses and sins, in which you once walked according to the course of this world, according to the prince of the power of the air, the spirit who now works in the sons of disobedience, among whom also we all once conducted ourselves in the lusts of our flesh, fulfilling the desires of the flesh and of the mind, and were by nature children of wrath, just as the others.

But God, who is rich in mercy, because of His great love with which He loved us, even when we were dead in trespasses, made us alive together with Christ (by grace you have been saved), and raised us up together, and made us sit together in the heavenly places in Christ Jesus, that in the ages to come He might show the exceeding riches of His grace in His kindness toward us in Christ Jesus. For by grace you have been saved through faith, and that not of yourselves; it is the gift of God, not of works, lest anyone should boast. For we are His workmanship, created in Christ Jesus for good works, which God prepared beforehand that we should walk in them.

Ephesians 4:19 (TPT)

> Because of spiritual apathy, they surrender their lives to lewdness, impurity, and sexual obsession.

Philippians 3:12–14 (NKJV)

> Not that I have already attained, or am already perfected; but I press on, that I may lay hold of that for which Christ Jesus has also laid hold of me. Brethren, I do not count myself to have apprehended; but one thing I do, forgetting those things which are behind and reaching forward to those things which are ahead, I press toward the goal for the prize of the upward call of God in Christ Jesus.

Colossians 3:1–3 (NKJV)

> If then you were raised with Christ, seek those things which are above, where Christ is, sitting at the right hand of God. Set your mind on things above, not on

things on the earth. For you died, and your life is hidden with Christ in God.

James 4:7–10 (NKJV)

Therefore submit to God. Resist the devil and he will flee from you. Draw near to God and He will draw near to you. Cleanse your hands, you sinners; and purify your hearts, you double-minded. Lament and mourn and weep! Let your laughter be turned to mourning and your joy to gloom. Humble yourselves in the sight of the Lord, and He will lift you up.

1 Peter 4:1–2 (NKJV)

Therefore, since Christ suffered for us in the flesh, arm yourselves also with the same mind, for he who has suffered in the flesh has ceased from sin, that he no longer should live the rest of his time in the flesh for the lusts of men, but for the will of God.

1 John 2:15–17 (NKJV)

> Do not love the world or the things in the world. If anyone loves the world, the love of the Father is not in him. For all that is in the world—the lust of the flesh, the lust of the eyes, and the pride of life—is not of the Father but is of the world. And the world is passing away, and the lust of it; but he who does the will of God abides forever.

1 John 5:11–12 (NKJV)

> And this is the testimony: that God has given us eternal life, and this life is in His Son. He who has the Son has life; he who does not have the Son of God does not have life.

FREEDOM PLAN:
PURSUE WHOLEHEARTEDNESS

Contemplate: Read Psalm 119:9–11. Describe to yourself what wholeheartedness looks like and what it would take to be this way with your pursuit of Jesus. Get specific as it relates to your life, your schedule, your unique situation. Pick one of the verses used in this chapter and take the time to write about what it means to you.

Answer: What does wholeheartedness look like to you? How would you define wholeheartedness?

What are five characteristics or traits of wholeheartedness you want to start pursuing today? Of those five, which one is of the highest importance, and how can you prioritize it in your life?

Are there any particular parts of your day, in the past, that compelled or enabled you to dabble with pornography? How can you strengthen yourself against that portion of the day or get help to fight the temptation?

What areas of your life would you consider weak in terms of your being wholehearted for Christ? How would you strengthen them?

Pray: Dear Father, my desire is to know You and learn from You. I have been a weakling regarding being Yours alone. I have given myself over to many other things and classified them as my priority. I have been soft in having clear lines of loving You fully. Please forgive me for this. Help me, Lord, to have You as my undivided pursuit, my focus, my daily desire. Lift me up to see You clearly. In Jesus's name. Amen.

FREEDOM PLAN:
SERVE THE LORD AND OTHERS

Contemplate: Take a time inventory during this week of your life. Journal moments where selfishness ruled over your day, either by your actions or simply by your thoughts. Maybe you got angry when something didn't go your way or frustrated that you had to pick up the slack of someone else at work or at home. List these selfish moments and write a corresponding servant response to consider for the future.

Answer: How would you define service or serving? Go beyond a dictionary definition. How would you explain it to someone? What examples would you use to define it?

What are three to five specific areas at home, at work, and at your church where you can commit to acts of service this next week? Track these to see if you followed through on your commitment.

Who is someone that you would classify as a servant? What are the three characteristics that stand out to you about this person that reinforces their servant lifestyle? How could these characteristics be transferable to you?

Pray: Jesus, please come to me now. I have been so selfish and thought everything revolved around me. The more I look at myself, the more I notice that I have become a selfish person, and my pornography use has only been gasoline thrown on the fire of my self-absorption. Lord, please turn my gaze away from myself and allow me to see You clearly. Help me to see service as a joy and a blessing and that giving is more fulfilling than pursuing my own desires.

FREEDOM PLAN: DEVELOP A NEW LIFE AND DAILY SCHEDULE

Contemplate: As you leave behind a life in pornography, which was based on lies, and begin to pursue a new life—or better yet, the life He established you to live—consider everything that goes into your day. Think about how you determine what is to be included in your day. Consider how you prioritize certain things over other things. Reflect on who else gets to speak about what your daily schedule looks like.

Answer: In your pursuit of freedom from pornography, what would a "perfect day" look like? Go hour by hour on a typical day and describe what that day would look like free from pornography and sexual diversions. If you followed the schedule of that "perfect day," how would you feel about yourself at the end of the day?

What do you want the new you to be like? What areas must you change and grow in to become the person you desire to be? How does the order of your day coincide with this?

Who are the people that you will invite into the scheduling of your day so that any blind spots are noticed and addressed or just to provide another perspective on how you use your time?

Pray: Holy Father, thank you for caring for me even when I have not cared for myself. Thank you for being a God of order and structure and offering those to me as well. The ways in which I have lived my life up to this point have not been good, and in many ways, they have been damaging. Please come into my life, every minute of my life, and show me how to live and how to make decisions. Your ways are perfect, and I need You.

FREEDOM PLAN:
SHARE YOUR STORY

Contemplate: As you begin to engage a group of others who are supporting your freedom, consider how important this is to your success. Take the time to really engage with these guys and hear their stories, not just you telling yours. Become comfortable over time with this group explaining your highs and lows, victories and defeats, and praying with each other. As you grow in your purity and in your comfort in sharing your story, feel free to expand your level of vulnerability with others, to the point where you can give your full testimony of overcoming pornography use.

Answer: Who are the two to four other men that you trust to invite into your secret? What is holding you back from contacting them today? That is not a hypothetical question, but a very real one! If you're not willing to do this right now, then why not?

What is it that holds you back from sharing your story with other men? Are you afraid of their response? Are you struggling with trusting others?

How would you describe "the power is in the secret"? How has this played out in your life?

Pray: Merciful Father, who has cared for me and loves me, thank You for being so near. Thank You for loving me in my worst days and when I ran so far from You. Your loving kindness to me is so precious and undeserved, and I thank You for giving it to me so generously. I ask You, Holy Spirit, to counsel my heart and give me insight into the sharing of the victories You have given to me. Jesus, please let my testimony be full of Your grace, and may it help others to find freedom in You too. I love You!

Printed in the United States
by Baker & Taylor Publisher Services

Printed in the United States
by Baker & Taylor Publisher Services